# "An Old Fashioned Church for a New Fangled World"

## The History of Mead Memorial United Methodist Church and It's Service To God.

Collected and Authored By:

# Sharon C. Whitt

Published by: Dahnmon Whitt Family

Copyright 2011 by Dahnmon Whitt Family Publishing

Post Office Box 831
Flatwoods, Kentucky, 41139
606 836 7997
Web site http://dahnmonwhittfamily.com/
c-dahnmon@roadrunner.com

ISBN 978-1-61364-920-6
Published December 12, 2011

## This is book number_____ of 1000

# This first section was researched and written by Reverend Larry Sears Nichols in 1980.

Used with his permission Sep. 1, 2011

## Preface

Even before my wife and I moved to Russell, Kentucky, in June of 1979, we heard of a rather peculiar situation. Here, within three blocks of each other, stand two relatively large United Methodist churches. Soon after our arrival we began to hear of past efforts to merge the two congregations. It turned out that, since 1939, such efforts were regularly being discussed. As many as a half dozen times in recent years some such endeavor has been attempted. One attempt after another ended in failure. A search for answers naturally developed. Appropriate questions needed to be asked and explored. This research is partially a result of the questions asked and the replies that were given. An effort has been made to assimilate the historical and sociological data and to arrive at some tentative conclusions.

The first Methodist Church at Russell was a frame building known as the Mead Chapel; the Mead family having been instrumental in building it. Henry Mead paid off a debt on the old church, and the new one, Mead Memorial, was named in honor of the family. Mrs. Belle Mead Prichard, who was born and reared at the mead farm, gave generously to the erection of the new church. (1)

This, then, is a piece of neglected and almost forgotten history. A glorious past, a part of the good old days, and a candid look at the successes and failures of past generations. This resurrection of the Mead Memorial United Methodist Church heritage is part of the raison d'etre of this research. Feelings run high and there is justified pride that flows from the people at Mead when they share the examples passed to them from their ancestors. Future generations will also be able to look back at the present congregation and see and respect the dedication exhibited to God and to the church at Mead. Yesterday were good days. Today is the good old days. Tomorrow will be better and the best is yet to come.

A second part of this research is a sociological analysis of the present congregation with comparisons and contrasts made between the two Methodist churches in Russell. An extensive questionnaire was developed and given to heads of leading families in both congregations. An exhaustive amount of personal interviews preceded and followed the formal questionnaires. In addition, a number of letters were written and received from five or six states providing little-known and much needed information. The far-reaching influence of one's primary socialization was observed as more in-depth research developed. Time-proven generalities were often confirmed, yet frequent exceptions also surfaced. My investigation resulted in some opposite conclusions from those of many of my predecessors in the ministry, particularly in reference to the Mead congregation. These will be more specifically outlined in my conclusion along with implications for the ministry. Let it suffice here to simply assert, without reservation, that there is not only room, but there is a real need for two Methodist congregations in Russell.

Very little of this research has been obtained from library bookshelves. Most, therefore, lends itself to be deemed original, especially in regard to the history. Careful attention has been given to put in quotations any oral responses to a specific question. Footnotes are short, the bibliography is brief, but the information gleaned is substantial and has particular value because it has collected data that probably soon would have been lost forever to future generations.

Footnote
(1) Nina Mitchell Biggs, History of Greenup County Kentucky (Evansville, Indiana: Unigraphic, 1975) Page 72

# Table of Contents

*Chapter* *Page*

Preface... ... ... ... ... ... ... ... ... ... ... ... ... ... ... ... ... .... 2

1. *Mead Methodist Church, Beginnings*... ... ... ...    6

2. *The Grand Revival of 1907 A Bigger Building Is Needed*... ... ... ... ... ... ... ... ... ... ... .... ... ...    8

3. *New Church Dedicated*... ... ... ... ... ... ... ... ... ....    9

4. *Revival and Healing 1927*... ... ... ... ... ... ...    16

5. *Differences Versed Between Baptist and Methodist*... ... ... ... ... ... ... ... ... ... ... ... ... .....    19

5. *The Great Flood of 1937*... ... ... ... ... ... ... ...    28

6. *Mystery Artist* ... ... ... ... ... ... ... ... ... ... ... ...    30

6. *A New Cornerstone is Laid*... ... ... ... ... ... ...    36

7. *Footnotes*... ... ... ... ... ... ... ... ... ... ... ... ... .....    48

8. *Stained Glass Windows*... ... ... ... ... ... ... ... ...    55

9. *Art Glass Fund*... ... ... ... ... ... ... ... ... ... ... ...    70

10. *Disbursements of March 7, 1910 & reports*.....    71

11. Program of Dedication (new building)............ 75

12. Officers 1935.......................................... 81

13. Pictures............................................. 92

14. Officials 1980...................................... 97

15. Poems............................................... 103

16. Pastors that have served at Mead Memorial......... 108

17. Administrative Council for 2012.................... 112

18. Modern times Restoration.......................... 114

19. Vision of the Church 2009......................... 116

20. Restoration of the Twenty-first century............ 114

21. Interview with Bill Lanham, a long time member. 117

22. Raymond Payne's 17 years at Mead................. 118

23. Statement from our Pastor, Larry Puryear......... 119

24. Dedicated to....................................... 120

# Chapter 1
# Mead Memorial Methodist Church

*The record from the Greenup County Court Deed Book states that on March 8, 1874, a Captain Anthony W. Carner and his wife, Henrietta R. Carner, donated lot number 13 in Russell, Kentucky for a Methodist Church South to be erected.*
(1) This lot was located at what is now Boyd and Houston Streets, in Russell. The Trustees the lot was deeded to were Henry D. McKnight, Luke Powell, Armisted H. Mead, John Nichols, and John Bartley.
(2) To a few of the older residents in the community the Mead Memorial United Methodist Church is still regarded as the Southern Methodist Church. Likewise, the First United Methodist Church in Russell (only three blocks away) is sometimes referred to as the Northern Church by some of the older people in the community. Some of the underlying economic and political heritage of the North-South confrontation can still be faintly traced from these roots to the present structures. On a number of occasions, primarily by those who are inactive in the churches or simply live in the community, I have been informed that the Mead Church is Democrats and the First Church is Republican. For a few, this is the explanation why two United Methodist congregations a few blocks from each other remain separate bodies. Others imply the gap is economical, while maintaining that the

congregation at First Church is more professionally oriented and also in higher income brackets.

Services for the Mead congregation were first held in a school house in what is now called Kenwood. The early Mead Church had two doors—one for men and one for women—and was white with red door and window frames. This Mead congregation was served by Circuit Riders for many years. The history and experiences of these early circuit riders can be gleamed from the book appropriately entitled, <u>Saddlebags Preacher.</u> (3) In the early days of Kentucky Methodism the Methodist people were often called the shouting Methodists because of the joyous and enthusiastic manner in which they worshipped, and these Saddlebag Preachers rode the fervor of the frontier and led the scattered congregations such as Mead to establish an impressive tradition. Some of the early Circuit Riders that served Mead Chapel were:

John T. Johnson, Hiram Moore, J. M. Lock, J. F. Medley, J. M. Carter, C. W. Shearer, and F. S. Williams.(4)

The first church building was of a frame construction. Built in 1886-87, it was called Mead Chapel. This frame building was erected on the identical site of the present sanctuary. Mrs. Helen Mead Young made what was believed to have been a donation of $100.00 toward the construction of the frame chapel. She reportedly sold a crazy quilt and gave the money to the congregation to start a building fund.(5) Among the first members, names were: Mr. & Mrs. Peter Trent, Miss Jennie Trent, Mrs. Naomi Foster, Miss Nannie Arnold, Mr. & Mrs. Samuel Simpson, Mr. & Mrs. Silas Weeks, Mr. & Mrs. Tom Chinn, Mrs. Lillie Murphy, Mrs. Emma Clancy, and others.(6)

# The Grand Revival of 1907

In 1907 a revival meeting was held by G. C. Hutchinson and Walter M. Givens. This resulted in more than 200 conversions, most of whom joined the church. (7) It was evident that the present structure was too small for such an expansion of membership. Plans were made to build the present house of prayer. The pastor, O. F. Williams, led the campaign. Many ice cream socials were held to raise funds for the new church building. A number of the townspeople were said to have joked that, "the building would fall as the foundation was built on ice cream". (8) The "Hattie Brown Sunday School Class" did quilting, made apple-butter, and served church dinners to help raise money for construction. The total cost of construction was twelve thousand, two hundred dollars. (9) A few of the members of the class were: Hattie Brown, Mary Hill, Emma Carey, Alice S. Riel, Amanda Short, Virgie McConhay, Martha Lanham, and Ned Smith. The money partially raised, the building was soon erected.

# New Church Dedicated

The dedication service was celebrated on Sunday, July 3$^{rd}$, 1910. (10)  At that time and before. The Mead congregation was called the First Methodist Episcopal Church, South.  The other Methodist church in Russell was simply called the Methodist Episcopal Church.  It was not until 1969 when the Evangelical United Brethren and The Methodist Church merged that the term United Methodist Church arrived.  Before this uniting in 1969, another joining of hands had taken place in 1939.

The dedication sermon was delivered by Bishop R. B. Waterhouse of Emory, Virginia.  He received an honorarium of fifty dollars. (11)  (Duplicate of the 1910 program is reproduced in the Appendix of this paper.)  The original cornerstone was donated by the Smith Lodge and included a Masonic emblem.

During this unique worship and dedication service an opportunity was again provided to each one to share in paying off the mortgage.  Mrs. Alice S. Riel, one of the early Sunday School Superintendents, gave an offering that was compared to the widow's mite event.  She had three young boys and her husband had died while the boys were quite young.  When the Bishop saw what this widow had given, he volunteered to give an equal amount in the name of each of her sons and thereby gave an additional challenge to the congregation.  The boy's names were Berkley, Lawrence, and Halsey.  Only a few years afterwards, the middle son, Lawrence, tragically drowned while on a fishing trip with his brothers.  He was eleven years old at the time of his death.  Mrs. Riel died in 1965.  Years later, the youngest son, Halsey, helped the other men place the bell in the tower. Halsey Riel, in later years, also traveled to Pickering's Hardware in Cincinnati and brought back the gong-type product on an early passenger train. This gong is now used to announce the ending of Sunday School classes and to prepare for the entire church's worship services. (12)

The close of the dedicatory service featured an unusual and joyous event. It was at this time that the wedding ceremony of Mr. & Mrs. Sam Siple took place. Mrs. Siple was a Simpson before she married. After their wedding the young couple moved just across the river to Ironton, Ohio, and made their home there.

After the construction of the church, additional indebtedness surfaced from the assessment of the streets being paved on three sides. Brother J. R. Mullins was pastor when Belle Mead Prichard of Charleston, West Virginia, made a liberal contribution, matching dollar for dollar with the Congregation. (13)

The church organist (reed) from 1907-1947 was Mrs. Lily D. Harden. One of the imported French windows above the choir loft bears her name. Her daughter, Sara Marie Arrington, was also one of the music leaders of the church. She taught the present organist, Lynn Wilson Dixon, and many others to play. Mrs. Arrington played for one of the morning worship services as late as 1979. (14) In 1946, Mrs. Elizabeth Warnick was chosen as Mrs. Hardin's successor, and she served in this capacity until 1948 when she transferred her membership to the First Methodist Church where she presently continues as a church organist. (15) During the late 1940s approximately

nineteen families transferred their membership to First
Methodist.

Most of the early ministers of the Mead congregation
demonstrated an avid interest in missions and missionaries.
Almost once every month a special sermon and worship service
was conducted on this particular theme.  The December, 1907,
records written by F. C. Hutchinson spell out the emphasis
when he wrote "we have preached three times on the subject of
missions".  Again in February of 1908, Pastor Hutchinson
writes, "we have endeavored to do what we could for the cause
of missions".  In 1909 under Pastor O. F. Williams the
optimistic report reads:  "Our Sunday School has kept pace wit
the times, and we are happy to say, has raised the assessment
for the Foreign Missionary claim".(16)  For a score of years,
one cannot help but notice the attention given to the mission
field by this congregation and its pastors.  Although early
written records are scarce, those that are available document
such concern.

Brother O. F. Williams introduced all of his written reports to
"Dear Fathers and Brethren."  When he wrote regarding "the
building of a new church on the site of the old one" he
recognized the difficulty that would surface to maintain orderly
worship services. For this reason the trustees were empowered
to sell the old building, and apply the amount received there
from to the erection of the new church. During the brief interval
that followed, some worship services were held in a nearby
movie theatre. Most of the written reports by O. F. Williams are
extremely difficult to read, ironically, however, one word
stands out in various places is missions. A number of financial

reports of the erection of the present church building in1910 can be read in the Appendix.

Brother C. A. Slaughter, who followed O. F. Williams, writes concerning the general condition of the church with particular reference to the finances when he states, "they are working hard for the riddance of the church from debt and their minds are chiefly occupied with which may account for the fact that not more attention is given to the more spiritual side of the life." In April of 1911 he continues and makes note of a goal of average of 150 for Sunday school at the very least for the next quarter. It was also reported that a large pulpit Bible was presented to the church by the Epworth League which was under the management of Mrs. C. A, Slaughter and Miss Ruth Smith. (17)

By June of 1911 the goal of 150 for Sunday school had been reached and the challenge was given to reach 200 followed by an affirmation "and we believe we will get it."

Brother Slaughter writes on the spiritual condition of the church:

*If I were asked to define in one word the spiritual condition of the church I should borrow from an old fellow who said, when asked how his sick wife was getting on, "She's jes so-so—jes" so-so!" The summer months bring on the influence of Sunday baseball, amusements and other gaieties which tell in some degree at least upon the spiritual atmosphere of the town and the church suffers there from. We are doing what we can however, to counteract these influences with prayer that God may lead us to greater victories through Christ Jesus, our living head* (16)

In 1911 Mrs. C.D. Gladwell joined the church while Percy Thornburg was pastor. It was in a Monday afternoon interview with Mrs. Gladwell that a portion of this early information was collected. The Thornburg's and their three children served the church from 1911-1913. Brother DeMaro was the able Sunday School Superintendent at this time. (19)

Despite a number of contagious diseases prevalent in the community, with measles being one that was singled out, the attendance and spiritual conditions were reported to be in good shape. Brother Thornburg writes too, regarding missions and expresses his belief when he insists, "the life and activity of the church depend in very large measure upon the missionary spirit of the church." He continues and closes his report on October, 1911 by praying, "The Lord speed the day when every Southern Methodist and friend of the church will work and pray for this great cause that is so near the heart of the Master." (20)

In January of 1912 Brother Thornburg records an increase in attendance in worship services over the preceding quarter. He adds that the attendance at prayer meeting had almost doubled from the beginning of last quarter. "No more important service is held than that of a live spiritual prayer meeting, for it is the life of the church," he insists. Approximately twenty were converted in their 1911 revival, and in addition, Thornburg writes, "its influence reached the home life to the saving of some at the home altar". He closes his report by, "praying and looking for greater things on and on, and may the time be not far in the distance when every one shall be interested in the Soul of his fellow man". (21) In the summer of 1912 it was recorded that from 700-800 people attended a special Children's Day service. (22) It adds that the house was crowded. From my figures and observations, I would guess they were sitting in the aisles, on the steps, around the altar, and leaning over the edge of the balcony. Shortly after this service of extremely high interest, all the churches had to close one Sunday because of Diphtheria. In only one quarter of 1912, Brother Thornburg reports forty-three additions to the church representing about twenty-three homes that had not previously been identified with the church. (23)

A. A. Hollister was appointed to the Mead charge in 1913. He had no children, although his nephews are still deeply involved in the Methodist Church in West Virginia. Apparently some of the zeal of previous years was fading slightly. In 1913, Brother Hollister reports, "we need more of the zeal that causes people to pray, study the Word, and attend the services of the church". He adds, "We have used our best efforts for finding those called to preach, but as yet none have decided to answer the call". In 1915, he continues, our Congregation is not as enthusiastic for missions as is good for their spiritual growth". (24)

I have not been able to obtain any information on H. K. Moore or his ministry at Mead from 1914-1916. The records are lost and no one living seems to remember much about him. However, the four years that J. R. Mullins served at Mead seemed to be a time of increased activity. Brother Mullins was a widower with three children. Two of the children's names were Robert and Rose. I was told that he was a handsome man and naturally received a lot of attention from the single women in the church. Many were said to have flirted with him and others made attempts to get him married. His hair was solid white with almost a silver tint. On one occasion, in preparation for a date with a maiden lady he had not yet met, he decided to reach for a younger look. He only meant to dab a small amount of brown dye on the side of the hair but he slipped and instead used entirely too much dye and the result was a full head of dark brown hair. The following Sunday as he entered the pulpit many of the parishioners did not even recognize him. He smiled and explained what had happened. The congregation was greatly amused. (25) Nevertheless, about a year later, probably in 1918, he married this maiden lady whom he had originally met covered with false pretenses.

In 1916, a resolution of thanks to Mrs. Emma Clancey for the gift of the parsonage was drawn up, and a similar resolution was offered to Mrs. Bell Prichard for a gift of one thousand dollars to go on the church debt. (26) This first parsonage was located directly across from the church and is now the home of Mrs. Carrie Hareless who is a member of the church choir. The present parsonage, some one mile from the church, was obtained in 1934. In 1917, a communion service was bought for the church by Mrs. Brown's class of women and during these years the first Sunday of each month was used to take the Sacrament of the Lord's Supper combined with the special training of the children. The last Sunday of each month was observed as missionary day. The average Sunday School attendance for these years was 150 with a Sunday School rally day in 1916 recording 194 in attendance. (27)

# Revival and Healing 1927

Revival breaks out again.  In March of 1917, the evangelist, A. M. Martin, was scheduled for a two-week revival.  Services started rather slowly.  For about nine weeks a young Mrs. Gladwell had been mysteriously paralyzed from the neck down.  She prayed and asked God to heal her so that she could raise her little girl.  Suddenly at two A.M. on Monday morning God instantly healed her of what was found to be, in 1938, a curvature of the spine and polio.  She promptly went to the services that were in progress.  The topic that night was "Removing the Stumps".  Seven stumps were numbered by the evangelist.  The first four missed their mark.  The last two were not even heard, however; stump five pierced her heart.  Of the seven stumps that hinder a Christian in the spiritual growth, it was the 'unforgiving spirit" (stump five) that brought conviction.  As "Just as I Am" was being sung, Mrs. Gladwell turned and saw her brother walking down the aisle.  She saw a halo type vision around his head.  She too walked the aisle rejoicing and praising God.  She prayed and while praying, shouting broke out among the entire congregation.  She went to that one with whom she was feuding, and they immediately embraced and gave thanks.  Scores of individuals were converted in the days that followed.  A number were called to preach and others to be missionaries.  It was said that after this revival it was no trouble to get Sunday School teachers and other volunteers for the work of the church.  By February of 1918, there were 300 students enrolled in the Sunday School classes. (28)

A. L. Spencer was the shepherd of the flock from 1920-1924.  In 1922, E. W. Potter became the Sunday School

Superintendent. His son, also a dentist, became a member of the First Methodist Church in later years. The records show that the Sunday Schools often had over 200 students present. On January 22, 1922, there were 228 in Sunday School at Mead. (29) Few other records have been redeemed from this period of mead's history. In 1920 or 21, the central stained glass window with Jesus holding a lamb in his arms needed repairs. The window was carefully removed from its frame and carried to the Ohio River. From there, it was placed gently on a ferry boat and taken to Ironton, Ohio. This was just before the bridge connecting Ironton, Ohio and Russell, Kentucky was completed (1822). A glass repair business owned and operated by a black family specialized in this type of work. One of the employees, a Mr. Andrew Johnson, did the work and the precious window was returned to the church. (30) Mr. Johnson's nephew and his wife now live in the Hillcrest-Bruce apartment complex in Ashland, Kentucky. The United Methodist churches have a valuable and worthwhile outreach within this government housing project. The full-time staff person who ministers there is Miss Fay Pickel. Miss Pickel is a member of the Mead congregation and is a very able and appreciated choir director for the church here.

Another black man with close ties to the church was Arthur Farmer. He was the custodian of the church facilities for a number of years, and he also worked at the Russell Railroad YMCA. He was described to me as a hard worker and a good man. One person told me that Mr. Farmer, his wife, and a couple of children would, on occasion, attend the worship services, but would sit in the back corner. Others do not remember those attending services, but do remember him and his son came here.  At the time of his work the church there was a huge gas chandelier in the middle of the sanctuary.  Mr. Farmer was known to extend a ladder from the balcony railing and lower it across a part of the light fixture, and then he would ease out on the ladder overlooking the congregation and light the wicks for worship services. (31)  A unique acolyte he must have been!

Brother Ivy Yoak was pastor during some of the depression years.  Brother Yoak and his family served the congregation here from 1924-1929.  His daughter, Miss Edyth Yoak, still attends church here and has been faithful to the work of the church for years.  Miss Yoak was also a school teacher in the Russell system and specialized in languages.  Brother Yoak received special recognition from the Kentucky Conference for collecting the balance of the superannuate fund which had been in arrears.  Also during his pastorate, a very spiritual revival was held by Brother E. R. Overly with C. H. Rayl as singer.  Each year a revival was held in the Fall and in the Spring.  In the late 1920's the high choir loft was lowered to its present height.  Before this time, the choir loft was lifted up much like the balcony.  There was a narrow set of steps leading up to it, but they provided only one way down.  In case of fire, routes of escape were limited and thus considered dangerous for the choir.  In addition, there were those who needed more room to play such instruments as a bass fiddle and a sliding trombone with the orchestra which accompanied the choir.  Dropping the choir loft nearer to the congregation seemed to be considered a very wise move indeed and the choir proved to be more effective. (32)

# Differences versed between Baptist and Methodist

I have discovered only one document connected with the ministry of John Brown (1929-1931). However, this one paper is of an interesting event and, therefore, I feel is worthy of reproducing in its entirety. This was written by John R. Gilpin, the pastor of the First Baptist Church in Russell. The public schools had asked to use the Baptist Church facilities for their Baccalaureate Services and had asked Brother Brown to be the speaker. The paper is entitled, "Why The First Baptist Church Did Not Permit The Baccalaureate Sermon To Be Preached In Their Church Building"! The paper in its entirety follows as written by John R. Gilpin:

*In the last three weeks there has been much discussion concerning the action of the First Baptist Church in refusing the use of the church building for the Baccalaureate service this year. The principle of fair play and candid frankness demands that we present publicly the reason for the action of the church. First, let it be understood, that the action of the church does not discriminate against B. F. Kidwell as the Superintendent of our Public Schools, nor any member of the Board of Education. Our church has gone on record as offering the Public School the use of our building for the Baccalaureate services at any time they may wish to use it, provided they furnish a minister of like faith and order, as speaker.*

*Likewise, the action of the church is not a personal discrimination against J. E. Brown, the pastor of the Mead Memorial Methodist Church, who is the Baccalaureate speaker this year. Since Mr. Brown became pastor in Russell, there has existed a sympathetic friendship between the writer and Mr. Brown. When the latter was in the hospital last summer, we even had special prayers in our public services for his recovery.*

*Then how can the action of the church be accounted for? Simply on the basis of the vast differences of doctrine of the Methodist and Baptist churches, as the two systems of religious teaching are well nigh opposing and divergent in every respect. I shall cite a few of the more conspicuous differences.*

1. *Requirements for church membership.*
   *Methodists ask those seeking to unite with them to experience a desire to be saved. I quote from the 1930 issue of the Doctrines and Discipline of the Methodist Episcopal Church, South, P. 14, Par. 3, "There is only one condition previously requires of thee who desire admission into these societies, a "desire to flee from the wrath to come, and to be saved from their sins." In contrast, Baptists believe in receiving no one who does not profess that he is already a child of God. We ask more than a desire to be saved—we ask that the applicant have already experienced a change of heart. This, of course, is following the example of the First Baptist Church of Jerusalem: "And the Lord added to them day by day those that were saved." Acts 2:47.*

2. *The mode of baptism. Methodists accept three modes for baptism leaving the choice to the discretion of the candidate. Quoting the Discipline again, p. 340.*

*"Then shall the minister take each person to be baptized by the right hand; and placing him conveniently by the font, according to his discretion, shall ask the name: and then shall <u>sprinkle</u> or <u>pour</u> water upon him (or, if he shall desire it, shall <u>immerse</u> him in water), saying: I baptize thee in the name of the Father, and of the Son, and of the Holy Ghost. Amen."*

*Baptists believe in one mode only—namely immersion. This was the method employed by John the Baptist; "A John also was baptizing in Aenon near to Salim, because there was <u>much water </u>there." John 2:23.*

*This was the method whereby Jesus was baptized: "And Jesus, when he was baptized <u>went up</u> straightway <u>out of</u> the water." Mt. 3:16. This was the mode practiced by the early Christians: "And he commanded the chariot to stand still: and they <u>went down both into the water, </u>both Philip and the eunuch: and he baptized him. And when they <u>were come up out of the water</u>, the Spirit of the Lord caught away Philip, the eunuch saw him no more." Acts 8:38, 39.*

3. *The baptism of infants. Methodists believe in and practice Infant Baptism. Read p. 323-327 of the Discipline.*

   *This Baptist rejects, since there is no command, example, nor precept in the Scriptures which teach Infant Baptism. Someone has said, "Three classes of Scripture which teach Infant Baptism; the first mentions babies, but does not mention baptism; the second mentions neither babes nor baptism,"*

*The Scriptural commands and examples demands that only believers be baptized. See Acts: 10:47; Acts 16: 30-34: Acts 18:8. Since no infant has the ability to believe with saving faith, we reject infants from the ordinance of baptism.*

4. *The Question of Communion. Methodist believes in what is commonly called "Open Communion." Quoting the Discipline again, p. 25, Par. 25, "The cup of the Lord is not to be denied to the lay-people: for both parts of the Lord's Supper, by Christ's ordinance and commandment, ought to be administered to all Christians alike." This means that all Christians, irrespective of denominational differences should be admitted to the Lord's Table. Baptists believe that this ordinance is for a local church only, and that even Baptists have no right to partake of the supper, except in the church where they may be members. This is fully in accord with the teachings of Scripture: "For we being many are one bread and one body." The "one body" means nothing unless it means one local church. Each church is required to exercise discipline over those who partake of the Lord's Supper. See Cor. 11:17-21. This would be a complete impossibility unless all communicants were members of one local church. Thus, instead of inviting all Christians to the Lord's Table, we invite only those, our Savior invites, namely, the members of each local congregation.*

25. *The security of the believer. Methodist teaches that one can be saved, and after justification, he can lose his salvation, and go to Hell. The Discipline says, Page 22,*

*Par. 18, "Not every sin, willingly committed after justification, is the sin against the Holy Ghost, and unpardonable." This implies though that some sins after justification are unpardonable.*

*Baptist believe that when one is saved, he is saved eternally and can never be lost by the sins he commits. Jesus said, "I give unto them <u>eternal life; and they shall never perish</u>, neither shall any man pluck them out or my hand. My Father, which gave them me, is greater than all; and no man is able to pluck them out of my Father's hand. John 10: 28, 29. The Scriptures state that nothing can separate the believer from Christ: "For I am persuaded that neither death, nor life, nor angels, nor principalities, nor powers, nor things present, nor things to come, nor height, nor depth, <u>nor any other creature, shall be able to separate us</u> from the love of God, which is in Christ Jesus our Lord." Rom. 8: 38, 39.*
*Sin can't separate us: "For sin shall not have dominion over you." Rom. 6:14. Satan can't separate us: "He that is begotten of God keepeth himself, and <u>that wicked one toucheth him not</u>." Jn. 5:18. The law can't separate us from Christ: Ye are not under the law, but under grace." Rom. 6:14. Even the believer can not take himself out of God's saving grace: "I will put my fear in their hearts, which <u>they shall not depart from me</u>." Jer. 32:40.*

*Thus the Baptist and Methodist position is seen to be directly opposite and contrary. Long years ago, Amos asked, "Can two walk together except they be agreed?"*

*Amos 3:3. Since we do not agree, but widely differ with Methodism, we can not step aside and bid them God-speed in the use of our pulpit. To do so, would endorse every precept which Methodists hold. This we can not do, for as John says, "He that biddeth him God-speed is partaker of his evil deeds." II John 1:11.*

*Accordingly, since we do not agree with the principles of Methodism we must maintain a position of separateness, which true Baptists have done for the past 2,000 years, since Jesus said, "I will build my church and the gates of Hell shall not prevail against it." Mt. 16:18.*

*"Through many dangers, toils, and snares, we have already come; Tis grace hath brought us safe thus far and grace will lead us home."*

*P.S. If you desire to know more of The People Called Baptists, "Come thou with us and we will do thee good." Don't fail to hear Sunday Night's Message: "Will There Be Anybody in Heaven besides Baptists?" Don't attempt to get this message second-handed; hear it for yourself! P.S. The pastor was not present the night the church by vote refused the use of our building for the Baccalaureate services. Accordingly, he takes this opportunity to present to the public the reason for the action of the church. We are indebted to Pastor J. E. Brown, of the local Methodist Church, for the use of his book, The Discipline", quoted herein. (33)*

Along with the records of John Brown's ministry, information on Brother E. H. Barnette have been lost or destroyed. Brother Barnette served from 1931-1933 and one source was found that simply recorded the Sunday School attendance (213) for Easter Sunday of 1933. (34)

W. H. Foglesong was the pastor from 1933-1935. From 1934 to 1935, sixty people were received into the church. A seldom recorded prayer meeting attendance was registered as forty-one on one Wednesday night in 1934. He writes in 1935, "Our people are the most loyal to their pastor and some of the most heroic work it has ever been our privilege to see was done in our recent revival meeting. The Bible read, personal work done, old grudges settled, and a number of people graciously saved."(35) During Brother Foglesong's service at Mead, a Church Year Book and Directory was published. A copy of the Directory listing all the church members in 1936-1936 is said to be in the new cornerstone.(36) In 1934 the church bought a commodious seven room parsonage in the Riverview Addition to Russell. The house was deeded to the church by L. R. Dingus and Grace Dingus on July 5th. The Trustees at that time were: J. F. Wright, C. D. Gladwell, H. T. Short, Curtis Smith, S. S. Hill, T. J. Agnew, D. F. Hendricks, and J. D. Sweet. (37) In February, 1935, it is recorded that "Mead paid more per capita for Benevolences than any church in the district save one and stood 4th in the entire conference." (38) The congregation at Mead still maintains this extra-mile giving spirit to the work of the church. On a number of occasions in the 1930's a special offering was taken for Morris Harvey College, now located in Charleston, West Virginia. In Mat of 1935, eighty-five dollars was sent to the school from the local congregation. (39) A number of the young people from Mead attended and graduated from this institution of higher education. Plans to add six new classrooms to the third floor of the building were made in 1935 and soon thereafter carried out. At the present time there is only one classroom on the top floor. This upper room is used by the youth. There is some disagreement in the church records concerning the purchase of a new bell that was placed in the church tower. One document that this was accomplished in 1935; however, on a copy of the bill of sale, September 19, 1940, is the recorded date. The bell and fixtures were purchased from Stuckstede & Bro. in St. Louis, Missouri at a total price of $260.68. (40)

# Great Flood of 1937

In 1937, while C. C. Lambert was pastor, the Ohio River came out of its bank and flooded the entire Russell Community. Many families were left homeless and much damage was done to the businesses, churches, and other buildings in the community. The Mead Church was on higher ground and did not receive the full impact of the raging waters. It was again the people of church who came to the front and offered their services to their friends in need. Mead was the center for the food, shelter, and communication efforts of the area. The American Red Cross made their temporary headquarters at the church and assisted the Christians in these social endeavors. (41) Mrs. Lillian Fouts Thompson shared the following incident with me. She was a telephone operator at the time and the building which housed the switchboard was under siege from the restless Ohio River. The waters reached the second story windows; the building began to sway and gently rock the foundations. At two o'clock in the morning it was clear the time to evacuate had arrived. Boats eased near the windows and a ramp-like plank connected the telephone operators to the men in the boats. Six operators slid down the plank to safety. They were taken to the Mead Church and served food and slept overnight among others who had sought refuge in the arms of the church. Three of the church women named who were there in these early morning hours were: Mrs. Maude Giles, Lily Hardin, and Miss Susan Davidson. (42)

Another unusual, but tragic, event that occurred during the 1937 flood involved the deaths of two young boys. The boys were riding their sleds down Raceland Hill late at night. A milk truck was making its rounds and the boys guided their sleds right into its path. Both died instantly. Because it was now the early morning hours and the flood waters still surrounded the funeral home, the bodies were taken to the Mead Church for the night. George Hendricks and some other men placed the two boys in a small room near the choir loft. This room has since been closed off and is no longer in use. The next day some of the same men lifted the two bodies into a boat and took them to the funeral home in this fashion. The waters were up to the second floor windows and the boys' bodies were simply slid through the windows. (43)

Shortly after the waters receded, it was obvious that the church was in need of repair. The waters had finally filled the basement and all happenings were moved to the sanctuary and other upstairs facilities. The cost of the extensive repairs on the church totaled over two thousand dollars. (44) The following year (1938) a new venture in cooperation was initiated. Part of these efforts was due to the flood damage and to pulling together of groups of people during this time. The first unified Daily Vacation Bible School was organized. The two Methodist churches, the Christian Church, and the Church of God were all involved. At this time, Brother O. P. Smith was appointed to serve the Mead congregation. (45) He stayed from 1938-1944 and was well respected by the entire church body. In 1939, the very first talks concerning the merge of the two Methodist congregations in Russell began. The nationwide merge of the Northern and Southern divisions of the Methodist Church no doubt played a large role in originating such discussion. Although there was some little talk, no serious action emerged at this time. For the next thirty years, off and on, talk continued, and, on occasion, some tension developed.

# Mysterious Artist

In 1939 or 1940, a beautiful dimension was added to one of the Sunday School classrooms in the basement. Sadly enough, the creator of these works of art is unknown. He did not sign his name and few clues have been discovered as to his identity. One source explained that this mysterious man was a drifter just passing through. He was staying at the YMCA a few days and in an informal conversation his artistic abilities were mentioned. All of my sources agree that J. A. Frazier paid this mysterious man a sum of money to do the work. Mr. Frazier was a Sunday School teacher and had a class of teenage boys. (46) The paintings are truly a sight to behold. They are approximately four and a half feet wide and nine to ten feet long. A large portion of three walls are filled with their splendor. The titles lettered under each painting are: "Changing Pasture", "Beside The Still Waters", and "The Flight Into Egypt". The painting, "Changing Pastures", includes one large boat full of sheep surrounded by three shepherds. In the foreground is another such boat with the sheep huddled around the care of their shepherds. The destination of both vessels is to greener pastures. This change of one field to a better one can be easily recognized as the part of the Christian message that deals with leaving this earth by way of death's door and entering through the gates of pearl which leads to eternal bliss. "Beside The Still Waters" is also an allusion to the relationship between a good shepherd and his needy sheep. Sheep are said to be afraid of running water so, in order to quench their thirst, a wise shepherd must lead them beside still water.  On occasion, the waters in this painting are referred to as the Jordan River.  If that be the case, it might be that the title given to it is not altogether appropriate.  Nevertheless, after a heavy rain, a few years ago, a faucet-like funnel of water poured steadily out of the wall.  The custodian promptly announced to the people: "the Jordan River's leaking!"(47)  The third piece of art entitled "Flight Into Egypt" is the most implicit reminder of the head of the Church.  Jesus, presented as a child, is the central figure.  Mary, portrayed in bright colors, is also brought to the front.  Joseph, holding a serving donkey, looks over the central scene of mother and child.  This Sunday School classroom has been filled to capacity.  A loving spirit is always present and the artistic environment is exquisite, thanks to Mr. Frazier and an unknown drifter.

From 1938 to 1944, Brother O. F. Smith was the highly regarded pastor of the church.  He is now retired and lives just off Route 60 near Rush, Kentucky in Boyd County.  His son, Orson P. Smith, Jr. is a radiologist at the Methodist Hospital in Louisville and teaches a Sunday School class at one of the large Methodist Churches in Louisville.  While Brother Smith was the minister a local option fight developed.  Brother Smith led the campaign for the dry forces.  A special service was held for about eight young men who entered the service during World War II.  Three of the young men who entered at that time were Brother Smith's son, George Hendricks, and Bill McCutcheon.  Bill McCutcheon now lives in Hollywood, California and has been seen in a number of movies and television shows. Mr. McCutcheon was wounded in battle and when he got home he looked up Brother Smith. He testified to his beloved minister how, while he was in the foxholes and fields of heavy military activity, his constant thoughts were of his times of worship at Mead Memorial Methodist Church. (48) With a number of the young men in the military, the Sunday School figures for December of 1944, were 72, 100, and 96, in attendance for three successive weeks. Mrs. C. E. Bratton served as Sunday School Superintendent at the time. (49)

Sherwood Funk and his family entered Mead's history of pastors in 1944. His widow now lives in Decatur, Georgia. Few records are available for his three years work in Russell. One note of significant contribution can be pieced together in terms of the musical aspect of the ministry. Brother Funk was the pastor when the first electric organ was installed. Soon afterwards a special donation by Dr. and Mrs. M. J. McGuire supplemented cathedral chimes to the glory of God. In addition to these music-oriented contributions, the present piano was provided for worship services in the 1940's. Mrs. Sara Marie Arrington, who taught music lessons for forty-eight years, also sold pianos for a number of years. She sold one to the church and donated the first fifty dollars for its purchase. (50) Finally, another attempt at merger of the two Methodist churches surfaced again. This one was more serious and committees were formed and recommendations were made. The committee vote at First Methodist was 15 to 5 in favor of the plan. Mead

Memorial's merger committee voted 13 to 8 against the merge. As a result of the action taken by Mead committee, the matter was not referred to the congregation for a vote. Had the proposed merger been approved, the First Methodist Church building would have been used by the combined congregations for religious services. (51) This accounts for the committees opposite voter returns. It is assumed by many that, had a decision been made to use the Mead Memorial Church building in the event of a merger, the voting results would have been just the opposite.

After Brother Funk moved on to Shinkle United Methodist Church in Covington, Kentucky, the very gradual decline of the church soon became more rapid. A number of controversies developed and emotions ran high. Brother R. R. Rose became the pastor from 1947 to 1953, and his actions at Mead were marked by both a number of achievements and a number of controversies. Mrs. Rose was very active in the music department and considerable achievements and controversy enveloped her as well. (52)

Brother Rose often quoted George Whitfield, he seemed to be sound in his verbalized theology, preached often on tithing (especially for those whom the church has honored with official positions), and his sermons covered a broad range of subjects and scripture; both Old and New Testaments.(53) These positive elements apparently were coupled with an aggressive, arrogant, opinionated, uncompromising, egotistical, personality.

Love, patience, and understanding did not seem to be in large supply during these turbulent years. Small disagreements grew, hostilities developed, and division of the body widened which finally cumulated in approximately nineteen families leaving the church. Most of them went to First Methodist; some, however, went to other denominations in the surrounding area. (54)

A few of the seeds that developed controversy were: the issue of merger, laying of a new cornerstone, the audio-visual sound system, the musical program, dismissal by board action of some in official positions, excessive preaching on tithing, a fist fight on the street involving the pastor and a church member, and in general, a number of personality conflicts and undiplomatic procedures. Much of the conflict within the church is reflected expressively in the church bulletins of the time. (55)

Among the more positive elements that took place during the late 40's and early 50's include: extensive building repairs, a very active youth program, and a large number of high quality films shown, as well as a number of individual accomplishments. On January 28, 1951, the church had a "Tither's Testimonial Service". On February 11, 1951, James Edward Poe was congratulated on having completed the requirements for the "God and Country" award. He has the honor of being the first Scout to receive this award in Greenup County. On April 3, 1951, thirteen men were present at prayer meeting. On July 3, 1951, there were forty-one at Wednesday night prayer meeting. Among this relatively good attendance were a number of young people. On occasion it was reported that there were more youth in attendance on Wednesdays than there were adults. This, it seems to me, has both its positive and negative aspects. Dr. and Mrs. M. J. McGuire donated a chimes amplifier system which was equipped with a record player and twenty-five splendid records. The church's budget gradually increased during these years. In 1952, the budget was recorded as $5,923.00. The financial budget soon climbed to almost ten thousand dollars. On March 16, 1952, a list of men in the armed services from homes in the Mead congregation included: Edward Bratton, Francis Byrne, J. T. McGuire, Ralph Hay, Gene Clark, Charles Homer, Bob Greenslate, Page Johnson, Donald Arnold, James Kidd, Paul Trainer, and Ted Clark. (56)

During these years another vote was taken regarding a merger of the two churches. This time it got out of committee and to both congregations. Again, the First Methodist Congregation voted in favor of merger, but the Mead Congregation turned it down. Once again, one of the major issues and differences was regarding where the services would be held.

# A New Cornerstone is Laid

The new cornerstone of Georgia granite was laid May 17, 1950, and contained the inscription, "Mead Memorial Methodist Church, 1887-1909". The following motion was made and signed by sixteen members of the quarterly conference:

*We, the undersigned, hereby move that our new cornerstone be accepted as is, both as to the stone itself and the lettering thereon; and that we commend the donor of the stone, Harry L. Meadows, for the excellent work done in the provision and installation of this magnificent cornerstone and that this entire transaction be hereby considered closed. This motion was decisively carried as were all other motions which were adopted by the conference.*
*A lodge inscription was omitted because it could not be truthfully said that a lodge laid this new stone when it did not. The word "South" was left off the new cornerstone because the national merger of three Methodist churches in 1939 took the name of just "The Methodist Church", instead of M. E. Church or M. E. Church, South .(57)*

From 1953 to 1956, Brother J. B. Hahn served as pastor. His tenure at Mead was less explosive. Attempts were made to heal old wounds. Some progress was made, but, to a tragically large number, the tension and divisions were taken to the grave. Brother Hahn's widow writes of "three good years at Russell". (58) While Brother Hahn was at Mead, the Sunday School Superintendents were

Mrs. Clara Lewis and later Mrs. C. E. Bratton. Mrs. J. E. Phelps continued as church organist, a position she first received when Mrs. Warnick transferred to First Methodist. Few records remain of church activities and outreach during these three years. (59)

In 1956, John K. Hicks was appointed to the charge. He served the congregation until 1960. Again, few records exist to document the work of the church. In reviewing the list of youth who were active in 1958, it is on a positive note that I can report a large percentage of them still are faithful to the church. The youth fellowship leaders were Mary Poe and Francis Jane Simpson. The goal established for Sunday School on Easter Sunday of 1958 was 200. In January of 1957, Dr. E. Stanley Jones spoke at the First Methodist Church in Ashland and several from the Mead Congregation attended. (60)

Albert Savage, Jr. received the call to Russell in 1960. For his four years the church seemed to be stabilizing from the difficult years of early 50's. A new lighting system was installed for the entire building, and this was no small undertaking. A number of combined services with the First Methodist Church were noted in the 1960's and this sharing together continued in the 1970's. Especially noted was the combined daily Vacation Bible School between the sister churches. On October 3, 1961, the pastor reported his activities for the preceding month. His report to the official board reads as follows:

*The Pastor's activities this month have included the following: One of a kind meetings + Youth Activities Week Follow-up, Speaker at WSCS Student Recognition Banquet, Speaker at Russell P.T.A., Ministerial Association, Methodist Men, District Missionary Rally, MYF Sub-District Meeting at Melrose, MYF Sub-District Council Meeting at Greenup, MYF Picnic, Speaker at Russell Rotary for Red Cross, one funeral in Lewis Co., Invocation at "Y" Membership Dinner; other activities: 2 class meetings, 4 bowling meetings, 12 home visits, 4 prayer meetings, 5 C&O calls, 1 Bellefonte Hospital call, led 3 MYF evening meetings, conducted four Morning Worship services, Evening Worship Service, and taught 4 Sunday School lessons, attended 5 Commission meetings, 2 visits, 2 visits to the Rest Home, mailed invitations to the entire membership and constituency for Holy Communion, attended 2 official Board meetings, attended one Conference Board of Education meeting in Lexington, took three days to fence the back yard of the Parsonage, and otherwise kept busy.*

Brother Savage continues in another report to the Board:

*Our purpose in being here is to see growth in all areas. Our policy is to be aggressive. Our power is the Almighty God of the Universe, who has given us the privilege of calling Him Father. Let us attempt great things for God-things too big to do in our own strength-for only then shall we be able to feel His strength.*

On March 6, 1961, total full members of the church were reported to be 224. Church attendance averages for the month were: Sunday School-84, Morning Worship-67, Evening Worship-29, and Prayer Meeting-16. Brother Savage further commented that these figures show an increase in every area except the Evening Service. The tentative budget for the year 1961-1962 was $8,300. The youth counselors who served during these years were Bob and Teresa Mitchell. (61)

In 1964, rather amusing incident took place. Brother Savage had wanted to widen the door to the kitchen for some time. He wanted it open so the ladies of the church would listen to the after-dinner speakers rather than wash the dishes. The ladies wanted it to stay as it was. After Brother Savage went to conference and found he would be moving the following week, he took decisive action. During the week he took it upon himself quietly to widen the door. The next day when the women went to the basement they were stunned to see the entire kitchen area exposed to the public. "Look what's happened to our kitchen", they exclaimed. Some of the men secretly were smiling. The braver ones were more open about it. (62) The doors were widened in a clever act of sabotage and the empty gap remains open to this day.

After Brother Savage escaped the rage of the women folk and was safely out of town, Brother Walter Applegate came to town. He ministered and shared with the people from 1964-1965. Brother Applegate graduated from Asbury Theological Seminary in 1964. The same year ha was commissioned a Kentucky Colonel. A year after leaving the Mead Congregation (1966) he was Runner-up Pastor of the Year in Kentucky. Presently, he is minister of the First United Methodist Church in Prestonsburg, Kentucky. He is also currently working on his Ph.D. degree in Theology. (63)

In 1965, Raymond King received the Mead appointment. He also stayed for only one year. In fact, it is reported that he left the church about one month before conference time. Several members remember his keen interest and apparent drive to be a missionary. It is believed by some he is now serving as a missionary somewhere in South America.(64) I have not been able to locate him as of this writing and have no germane records of his efforts at Mead.

Ronald J. Masters received the appointment in 1966 and although he, too, was here for only one year, a little information concerning his ministry is available. The most recent Church Directory publication was completed during his year at Russell. A photograph of the beautiful church building graces the cover. Inside the front cover, the message from the pastor concludes: "This directory is just another way of saying that this is your church where EVERYBODY IS SOMEBODY". An extremely brief and gapped history of the church follows. This is followed by the various classes and groups within the Congregation. The groups listed and photographed include: Official Board, Choir, Hattie Brown Class, Men's Bible Class, J.O.Y. Class(Jesus first, Others second and Yourself last), Darlington Bible Class, Margaret Brasch Class, Happy Helpers, Methodist Youth Fellowship, Junior Class, and the Primary Class. There are thirty-six different photographs presented which include seventy-seven individuals within the frame. An even 100 last names and addresses are listed in the index. On the inside back cover is a list of the pastors serving the church from 1907-1966. (65) Brother Masters is now serving the Christ United Methodist Church in nearby Ashland, Kentucky.

O.M. Simmerman, Sr. pastured the church from 1967-1969. His widow also lives in Ashland at this time. Brother Simmerman's son and namesake presently serves the First United Methodist Church in Somerset, Kentucky. This is the church in which I (Rev. Larry Sears Nichols) was raised and had membership. During his years at the church some of those in official positions include: John Hill – Church School Superintendent, Mrs. J.E. Phelps – Organist, and Miss Lynne Wilson – Pianist. Bill and Sharon Lanham, Miss Brenda Nostrant, and Miss Macky Meadows all served as youth counselors. (66)

Ten years after Brother Simmerman's appointment (1977) his great nephew, Ludwig L. Weaver, Jr., followed his uncle's footsteps to the door of the pastor's study.

Another one year ministry began in 1969. The pastor appointed at that time was Paul Pepoon. He is described as having a peculiar personality and being somewhat aloof and introverted. Before his appointment he had been a guest speaker at one of the Methodist Men's meetings. The subject and content of his speech included specific and narrow views concerning sexual intimacy between married couples. Let it suffice to say that he had incurred the suspicions of the men before he ever arrived as pastor.(67) Evidently the feelings were never overcome, thus resulting in a brief one year stay.

Eston Calvert replaced Brother Pepoon in 1970. Brother Calvert speaks very highly of his experiences and friendships made during his four years at Mead. "People such as Cliff and Pauline Simpson, the Shafers, and Boll and Sharon Lanham mean much to me", he states. Brother Calvert entered the Navy during World War II and served in the Medical Department. After his discharge, he enrolled at the University of Cincinnati in Pre-Med. He finished his seminary work at Candler School of Theology in Atlanta, Georgia.

In writing of his ministry with the congregation, Brother Calvert mentioned the most difficult event that took place. Again this involves the attempt of merger. The District Superintendent, Kenneth Clay, felt very strongly about it. Once that the First Church was willing, but the Mead Congregation wanted to remain separate. Apparently the lines of division again centered around which church building would be used. The move to merge failed again. A significant contribution to the church and community from Brother Calvert was his role in establishing church basketball and softball leagues. This helped develop cooperation between denominations and within denominational lines. In fact, it was not long before the First and Mead Congregations merged their softball teams into one.

While at Mead, Brother Calvert had a number of health problems, including the removal of a kidney. He writes: "During this period I found a wonderful relationship and special feeling for Mead Church." His last year as minister at Mead was 1974. In 1976, Brother Calvert received an honorary Doctor of Divinity degree. And in July of 1978, he went blind while in the pulpit. After surgery on both eyes and a number of other health problems, Brother Calvert retired from the active ministry in June of 1979. (68)

In 1974, Leonard Sumner was appointed pastor. He served until 1977. One of the big events during his years was the Russell Centennial celebration. The church and church members tool a very active part in this joyous occasion. Tours were conducted of the church building. Dinners were served in the basement. Special events of all types and description were held in the community. Souvenirs were sold and distributed; sight-seeing trains rode the tracks again. Many tourists and visitors took advantage of this week-long celebration. The Mead Memorial Church drew special attention due to its prestigious history and unique facilities. The church's location, directly adjacent to the railroad tracks, also made it one of the most popular places for the tourist to visit.

Brother Sumner reports a spiritual awakening among the youth while he was here. He recalls twelve conversations and adds that ten of these were baptized. Another event he recalls involves an outdoor wedding. Those who attended thought it was very impressive. It took place on the farm of a nationally known Kentucky author, Mr. Jesse Stewart. Jesse Stewart is a member of the Greenup United Methodist Church only about five miles from Russell,

After three years at Mead Memorial the Sumners moved to the Olivet and Orange Charge in the Maysville District. While they served this two point circuit, Mrs. Sumners condition gradually grew worse. The Conference Board thought they should retire because of this situation. They are now living in their own house in Flemingsburg, Kentucky. After having preached the Gospel for twenty-two years full-time and ten years part-time, Brother Sumner writes: "We are thankful to have been privileged to preach the Gospel as long as we have—even now it is often my happy privilege to preach and fill in for my ministering brethren." He closes his letter, "Yours in the bond of Calvary." (69)

In 1977, Ludwig L. Weaver, Jr. was appointed by the Bishop to the Mead Memorial Charge. Lud and his wife, Jean, both have Master of Divinity degrees from Princeton Theological Seminary. They stayed for two years in Russell and presently serve as co-pastors of Salem and Grace United Methodist Churches and Campus Minister at Northern Kentucky University. While at Mead, Jean helped Lug develop the children sermon program and headed the Chrismon Tree Project. Both of these new efforts are still going strong and are greatly appreciated by the congregation. During this time, Miss Fay Pickel became the choir director. She recently joined the church and her contribution and her presence are greatly appreciated by all of us. Fay writes on January 1, 1980, "One of the best things that happened to me in 1979 was becoming a member of Mead Church! It is so great to have your concern, love, and support!"

Lud reports on his two years in Russell as his first Full-time church. He summarizes his goals and achievements as follows:

*When I arrived the church was in a state of decline that had been progressing for approximately three decades. My goal was to stabilize the church spiritually, physically, and financially. One of my areas of concern was church administration. An administrative board meeting had not been held in over a year. In the two years I was there we re-organized the church into committees and boards to meet regularly. We restructured the church school, dividing the classes so there would not be such wide age spans. We recruited six new teachers out of a total of nine, plus founded a subcommittee that organized a lab training school in the Ashland District in an effort to provide instruction for all our teachers.*

*We restructured our senior youth program, finding fifteen adults that would meet with the youth on a rotating basis. We also began a junior high school youth fellowship. A children's sermon was started in the Sunday morning worship service that succeeded in making the children feel more a part of the worship hour.*

*A number of new programs were initiated, such as Sunday evening church dinners, that went a long way towards promoting fellowship and bringing in some of our less regular members. I found a choir director and the choir performed a Christmas and Easter cantata. We inaugurated special services such as Christmas Eve, a Watch night Service, and a New Year's Eve party.*

*The physical plant of the church was in a stare of disrepair. We renovated the manse, doubling its value. Numerous repairs were made on the church, some major and some minor. Leaks and storage areas that had been ignored for twenty and thirty years were fixed and renovated. Every Sunday School classroom had some work done on them, from painting and carpeting to new lights and the installation of electrical outlets. Two new rooms were brought into existence and a volunteer nursery constructed, staffed and furnished.*

*Financially, two programs were conducted during my two year tenure. We participated in a Pension Crusade for the Kentucky Conference of the United Methodist Church. Our assigned goal was $4,600.00. The congregation pledged $10,211.00, more than double the goal. (70)*

In June of 1979, I (Rev. Larry Sears Nichols) was appointed by the Bishop to Mead Memorial. Wanda and I moved to Russell on the day of our tenth wedding anniversary (June 15, 1979). Wanda, Joshua, and I have been warmly received, graciously helped, and richly blessed during these six months. Many of the people are becoming actively involved in reaching up to God and reaching out to others. A number from Russell Convalescent Home attended services regularly. They also have been warmly received and their presence each Sunday and Wednesday never fail to encourage and challenge the congregation. They fold the church bulletins each Sunday and greatly appreciate this opportunity to feel useful and important.

The greatest joy for me during the past few months has been to be nearby when a number of individuals have received Christ as their personal Savior. Six men, three women, three boys, and nine girls have recently made such decisions. In addition to these first-time commitments, several others have come to the altar under deep conviction to pray and rededicate their lives. Six others have asked to transfer their membership from other denominations to the Mead congregation. The

Lord is bringing a harvest and we are all rejoicing together.

# Footnotes

1. Deed in the Mead Memorial safety deposit box at the First & Peoples Bank in Russell, Kentucky.

2. Ibid.

3. Interview on file with Mrs. Florence Ashley. Home movie in personal possession of the author.

4. Mead Memorial Church Records on file in the office. Filed under Church History.

5. Ibid..

6. Ibid.

7. Ibid.

8. Ibid.

9. Ibid.

10. Ibid.

11. Ibid.

12. Interview with Halsey and Grace Riel of Russell, Kentucky, October and November, 1979.

13. Mead Memorial Church Records.

14. Interview with Sara Marie Arrington, November, 1979.

15. Interview with Mrs. Elizabeth Warnick, December, 1979.

16. Mead Memorial Church Conference Records. Filed in the bottom file drawer in large hardcover journals in church office.

17. Ibid.

18. Ibid.

19. Interview with Mrs. C. D. Gladwell of Flatwoods, Kentucky, December, 1979.

20. Mead Memorial Church Conference Records.

21. Ibid.

22. Ibid.

23. Ibid.

24. Ibid.

25. Interview with Mrs. C. D. Gladwell, December,1979.

26. Mead Memorial Church Conference Records.

27. Ibid.

28. Ibid.

29. Ibid.

30. Interview with Halsey and Grace Riel, November, 1979.

31. Ibid.

32. Mead Memorial Church Conference Records.

33. Letter written by John R. Gilpin, pastor of the First Baptist Church, Russell, Kentucky. Written in 1924 And a copy is on file in the church office of Mead Memorial United Methodist Church.

34. Mead Memorial Church Conference Records.

35. Ibid.

36. A copy is in the Mead Memorial safety deposit box at the First & Peoples Bank in Russell, Kentucky.

37. Deed in the safety deposit box at the First & Peoples Bank in Russell, Kentucky.

38. Mead Memorial Church Conference Records.
39. Ibid.

40. In safety deposit box at the First & Peoples Bank in Russell, Kentucky.

41. Interview with Mrs. Lillian Fouts Thompson, December, 1979.

42. Ibid.

43. Interview with George Hendricks of Russell, Kentucky, January, 1980.

44. Mead Memorial Church Conference Records.

45. Interview with O. P. Smith, former pastor, January, 1980.

46. Interview with Sara Marie Arrington and George Hendricks.

47. Interview with Ray Shafer of Russell, Kentucky, October, 1979.

48. Interview with O. P. Smith, January, 1980.

49. Mead Memorial Church Conference Records.

50. Interview with Sara Marie Arrington.

51. Newspaper clipping in the safety deposit box at the First & Peoples Bank in Russell, Kentucky.

52. Interviews with a number of present church members as well as past church members.

53. Bulletins on file in church office under Church History.

54. Interviews with a number of present church members, as well as past church members.

55. Bulletins on file in church office under Church History.

56. Ibid.

57. Newspaper clippings in the safety deposit box of the First & Peoples Bank in Russell, Kentucky.

58. Letter from Mrs. Hahn. On file in church office under Church History.

59. Bulletins on file in church office.

60. Ibid.

61. Mead Memorial Church Conference Records.

62. Interview with Bob Mitchell of Flatwoods, Kentucky, January, 1980.

63. Letter from Walter Applegate under Church History.

64. Interviews with some members of the Mead Congregation.

65. From the latest church directory (1966). On file in the church office under Church History.

66. Bulletins on file in church office.

67. Interview with a church member.

68. Letter from Eston Calvert. On file in church office under Church History.

69. Letter from Leonard Sumner on file in church office under Church History.

70. Letter from Ludwig L. Weaver, Jr., on file in church office under Church History.

# Stained Glass Windows

Downstairs in the sanctuary—starting on the far right as one looks out from the pulpit and moving from right to left.

1.　　　Given in memory of William and Rosetta Brown by their son, this window has a wealth of symbolic meaning found within a faded blue circle. In the center of the circle is the cross, perhaps the most meaningful and significant reminder of God's love, the shed blood of Christ, and our redemption. The words faith, hope, and charity taken from I Corinthians 13:13 are engraved within rectangular shaped sections of ribbon. At the foot of the cross is the opened Holy Bible and protruding from the Scriptures is an anchor. This anchor represents hope as described in Hebrews 6:19. Similarly, the state of Rhode Island recognizes as its motto," Hope", and on the State flag is the anchor. The Bible, the anchor, and the three separate words (faith, hope, and charity) are all joined together by the interwoven ribbon that is wrapped around the cross. Here unity of purpose and the theme of the parts making a whole is stressed.

2.  Given in memory of J. S. and Ann Cliza Van Pelt by their daughter, this window is more simple in design, but contains a clear and significant message. Again there is a circled blue field with the primary figure being the dove. Two basic Christian meanings of the dove is to represent peace and/or the Holy Spirit. The representation of the dove as a peace symbol can Be gleaned from both the Old and New Testaments. In the dove's beak is an olive branch – another reminder of peace. Much of the origin of this Window can be discovered in the account of Noah and the flood. There are eight olive leaves on the branch; however in my research I have not been able to arrive at any explanation for this particular number. On the back of a United States one dollar bill, there is an eagle. In one claw the eagle is holding an olive branch with thirteen leaves and thirteen olive berries. In this case, the number thirteen represents, of course, the thirteen original colonies.

3.  This window is simply inscribed "Mary E. Huddleston 1824-1907" across the bottom. A harp is setting upright amid a sprig of palm leaves. Again, reference to both testaments is obvious. The Palm leaves are generally recognized as representing joy and victory just as the willow branch represents despair and defeat.

4.     The fourth window is inscribed W. F. Smith (1861-1897) at the bottom. The symbolic section of the stained glass contains an equilateral triangle with a dove flying across and down from the top of the triangle. Again, the dove brings emphasizes to the Holy Spirit and in this case, the Holy Spirit is coming down. The equilateral triangle is an early symbol of the church for the trinity—Father, Son, and Holy Spirit.

5.     "Naomi Mead-Foster (1840-1898)" graces the Window to right of the stained glass replica of Jesus. Above her name and encircled, as are all of these, is a large, upright rock standing stable in the midst of the sea. At the high point of the rock stands the cross. Around the cross a circle of rays are emitting light. Jesus is the rock in the middle of a sea of life (I Cor. 10:4). We are instructed to build our house on the rock first, because all other ground is sinking sand.

6.     This exquisite window is appropriately in the center of the sanctuary and is flanked by five other works of art on either side. The name recorded at the feet of Jesus is Birdie F. Cobbs. The entire window space is used in this one window to present the Savior of the world—Jesus Christ. He is shown here as the Good Shepherd. He carries a lamb in his right arm and is embracing this lamb close to his heart. The lamb is apparently looking up to Jesus and Jesus' compassionate eyes are fixed upon the lamb. In the left hand of Jesus is a shepherd's staff and His robe is

a bright red, covered with a purple shawl. This shoeless, bearded, long-haired image as a Shepherd stands out purposely as the showplace of all the rectangular windows in His church. The message is clear and simple—Jesus and His love shines forth. When the sun is shining brightly on a cold winter's day, the light from the stained glass windows lights and warms the sanctuary and the center of this light is this figure of Jesus.

7. Next to the "Good Shepherd" window is one in memory of "Chapman C. Cobb (1862-1907)". This window is distinguished by having a small Cross Pattee on top of the central area of a larger cross. Both are upright, and the larger cross penetrates a crown.

8. "F.G. Gooch (1867-1902") adorns the name plate at the bottom of this window. The message at the top contains an open Bible, a cross on top of the Bible, and a crown on top of the cross. Here we are reminded not only of the Scriptures which record parts of the life and message of Jesus, and the cross that reminds us of his suffering and love; but we are finally given recognition that Jesus is King. Indeed, He is the " king of Kings" and to Him every knee shall bow.

9. The inscription on window number nine reads "George Hill (1884-1903)". A Bible is not only closed, but apparently locked by a metal bar securing

the two covers in the middle. A lamp is resting on top of the Bible and a flame carries forth power and light. Many of the deeper messages contained in God's Word cannot be understood unless the Holy Spirit interprets these to the individual's heart and mind. It is the Holy Spirit who is the only true interpreter of the Holy Scriptures.

10.     This window gives only the name, "W. G. Whitt," at the bottom. Again, the honored Christian symbol of the cross stands prominent. The cross positioned up right penetrates the center of the crown.

*About W. G. Whitt:*
*By; Dahnmon Whitt, (A member at Mead Memorial United*
*Methodist Church,) had wondered if this W. G. Whitt could be*
*of kin. He went researching to see who this W. G. Whitt was*

*that Donated this lovely stained glass window way back in*
*1910.*

*His name is Woodson Gearheart Whitt the son of John Bunyan*
*Whitt JR. from Floyd County, Ky. Woodson was the youngest*
*child born 5 Feb 1859.*

*John Bunyan Sr. was a brother to Dahnmon's G.G. Grandfather, Jonas Whitt who settled in Greenup County, KY. in the 1840's. Woodson is Dahnmon's 2nd cousin two times removed.*

*Woodson left Floyd County to come to Russell to work on the railroad. He became a supervisor for C & O railroad and later became a police judge for the City of Russell, KY.*

*Woodson married Hannah Williamson and they had 2 children. Netty M. Whitt was born in Fort Gay, WV on 13 May 1883, and Jesse R. Whitt, (Female,) was born in KY in Aug. 1887.*

11.     A kneeling lamb supporting a crusader's flag introduces a worshipper to the sanctuary. Once again, the cross is highlighted as its message spreads across the entire width of the banner being lifted up. The inscription at the bottom reads "A. & O. B. Campbell."

12.     Behind the choir loft, there are three stained Glass windows. They are evenly spaced and high on the wall, they contain symbols of singing and praise to God.

13.     Facing these three windows, one's back would be exposed to the pews in the sanctuary. To the left of the center window can be seen three vase-shaped horns. These resemble the amplifier attached to the

old type victorola . There are a large number of leaves surrounding three sides; the three instruments of praise, "Lily D. Harden & Susan M. Davidson" is at the bottom.

14.    On the bottom right of the middle window is another harp. "Lexius Chinn (1875-1911)" is the name and inscription at the bottom.

15.    In the vestry downstairs are stationed two more windows. These were donated by the nearby Smith Lodge. Both windows are engraved "Smith Lodge # 775 A.F. & A. M." The symbols are of Masonic origins. The one coming up to the first floor is the Masonic "G" enclosed in a frame and sitting atop a rock that is surrounded by water. The "G" is surrounded by three candles. On top of the frame is something that appears to be a book. To the left of the rock is a streak of lightning zigzags across the sky. Something that looks like a small brown boat is in the far left corner. This window also has a small hole in it about one and one half inches long and one quarter inch wide.

16.    The window going on toward the balcony has an open Bible with the words "HOLY BIBLE' written across the pages. On top of the Bible is the Masonic emblem "G" with the traditional Masonic enclosure. Smith Lodge was chartered October 17, 1906.

17.   Going half-way up the steps one encounters two simply designed windows. The first one is in honor of "John B.Long (1830-1881)". Pictured in the upper portion of the window is a flying dove with an equilateral triangle in the background.

18.   The other window at this junction has "John B. Stevens (1840-1885)" at the bottom. The top half simply has an upright cross encircled with a dark blue background.

19.   At the top of the steps is a small hallway with two more unique pieces. As you reach the top, the window on your immediate left shows a Viking-type ship with the letters "T-B-H" formed on the full blown sail. The group identified on the bottom part is the "Tribe of Ben Hur.

20.   The other window in this hallway is a mystery to me. There is an anchor on the bottom left, however, the anchor lies on the ground. There appears to be a large X on the right. This X could be an hourglass. A podium is in the center and lifted up. There are three steps at the bottom of the podium and resting on top is an open Bible. The words "HOLY BIBLE' are inscribed along the top of the open pages. To the right of this pulpit is a flying dove with apparently an olive sprig in its mouth. To the left is an ark-like boat floating in the waters. This window, full of symbols, was donated by "Russell Lodge #36 I.O.O.F.".

21.    The balcony area contains eleven small stained glass windows and one large, round Rosetta Window in the center.  This Rose Window is an exact replica of the larger one that can be seen in the prominent Notre Dame Cathedral in Europe.  The first window describes herein is located to the far left facing the pulpit and choir loft.  This one given in honor of James Swearingen has a brown cross, an open Bible near the foot of the cross, under the Bible an anchor protrudes out both ends, and a ribbon containing the words, "FAITH, HOPE, and CHARITY" winds around the cross.

22.    Next to the James Swearingen window rests the Elizabeth Swearingen contribution.  The top of this window contains a floating ark and a flying dove overhead.  The dove seems to be flying toward the ark.

23.    The next two windows have blank spaces at the bottom where the names appear on the other ones.  This first one has the Rose of Sharon known as the Savior's Flower.

24.    This no-name window has one open lily and one closed Lily.  Above these two windows and enclosed in the same wooden frame is a colorful flower-like design with eight oblong petals.  Between and amid these petals are eight diamond-shaped pieces of glass.  These diamond shaped objects are all bright red.  This part is also called the small rosetta window.

25.     The Rosetta Window is very difficult to describe. It needs to be seen. Briefly, it is shaped like a wheel and has twelve wooden spokes as part of the frame. Between each wooden spoke is a panel of stained glass. There are twelve of these panes and all are bright and colorful with identical designs. There is a large four leaf clover design in the middle and this too is enclosed with a wooden frame.

26.     The next two windows are similar to the two on the other side of the Rosetta Window. This first one contains the title "Young Ladies" on it, but the next one is blank. This one has two bunches of grapes attached to a small twig which also has three leaves attached to it. The cluster of grapes signifies entry into Canaan.

27.     This window has an open lily and a closed one almost identical to window 24. Above these two windows is another design which is identical to the design above window 23 and 24.

28.     The next window was donated by Eastern Star. The five-pointed Eastern Star symbol is in the upper portion. The Mistletoe Chapter, which paid for this window, was organized in 1909.

29.     The "Washington Lodge #55" window has an elaborate design. A shield and a piece of armor are centrally portrayed. On each side of the armor is a broad ax and around the shield are the letters "F-B-C". On a

rectangular design below the shield are the words "KNIGHTS OF PYTHIAS". There is a small bullet hole in the center of this window. Apparently the shot was fired from the outside.

30.    On the side section of the balcony three additional windows were placed. The first one was in honor of "Kathryn C. Smith". The top half holds an urn. Two flaming candles make an X-like pattern in the background. On top of the lid of this urn is a small cross. The urn is symbolic for immortality.

31.    The middle window is on memory of "Eliza Arnett (1842-1900)". The anchor of hope is featured on the upper half enclosure.

32.    The third window in this section of the balcony was in memory of "B. V. & M. G. Kilgore, By Son". It has a large open Bible with the symbolic design and the words "HOLY BIBLE" written across the open pages.

33.    At one time where were six Sunday School rooms on this level of the church building. Now there is but one large classroom and this room contains three large and unique stained glass windows plus two smaller ones. The first large window has two separate circled designs. The one nearest the floor shows an open hand, possibly representing the hand of God. "The three extended fingers suggest the Holy Trinity, while the two closed fingers denote the two-fold nature of the Son."(1)  It is

possible some other meaning is intended, however, because this is a left hand and God is usually portrayed by a right hand, this seems unusual. The top section of the window features a crown—most likely the crown of life. Appropriately, this window was donated by the "Helping Hand" class.

34.     The middle window is in honor of the "B. F. Chinn Family". The bottom design has two equilateral triangles, one on top of the other. One triangle points up and one points down. The words on the one pointing up are "FAITH-HOPE-CHARITY". Around the triangle are three large circles. Each circle contains twelve smaller balls and the triangle pointing down also has twelve smaller circles within its boundary. The twelve represented in a number of windows probably meant to represent the twelve tribes of Israel.

35.     The final large window was given by the "Home Mission Society". A bundle of wheat is tied neatly together in the bottom circle. This is symbolic for the Feast of Pentecost.(2) The top circle is a replica of the scales of justice as presented on the front of United Stated paper currency. The scales signify the Final Judgment Day.

36.     The money for this window was donated by another Sunday School class called the "Willing Workers". It has a large flying dove encircled in the upper portion.

37.     This window was also given by the "Willing Workers". A darkened beehive is pictured in the top half. This

partially symbolizes that God's Word is sweeter than honey. It is also "a symbol for a community of those who work together for the benefit of all".(3)

38.    There are three windows in the pastor's study. The first one, given by "Mrs. J. C. Fulk", has a cross passing through the center of a crown.

39.    Located beside the preceding window is another one with the identical cross and crown symbols. This one was given by Mr. J. C. Fulk. The cross and the crown symbolize the reward of the faithful in the life-after-death to those who believe in the crucified Savior (Rev. 2:10).

40.    The third window in the study is in honor of "Clancy Mead deMar". The symbolism in this one is another open Bible with the words "HOLY BIBLE" spread across the top two pages.

41.    There are two final windows in a Sunday School room just off the pastor's study. Both of these rooms are near the sanctuary. The first window is in honor of "Seldon S. Stone (1838-1905)". This window has an open Bible with a crown on top and a cross penetrating through the crown. The word "HOLY" is across the left hand page of the Bible. On the right, only the letters "L" and "E" are visible. Presumably, the "BIB" is covered by the cross.

42.    The final small window covered in this list is in memory of "Rev. E. S. Williams,(1827-1884). He is the only

ordained minister thus honored.  Strangely enough, the Bible symbolized in this window is closed and latched. There is an old type lamp on top of the Bible and a small flame of light is coming out of this lamp.

43.    There is one larger Rosetta Window on another side of the building.  This window is the only one that cannot be seen from the inside.  From the outside it appears to be quite similar to the one previously described.

> 1.  Carroll E. Whittemore, Symbols of the Church (Nashville: Abington, 1959

> 2. Ibid

> 3. Ibid

# Art Glass Fund
### Total to March 7, 1910

| | |
|---|---|
| Mrs. J.C. Fulk | $15.00 |
| Mrs. W.A. Brown | $25.00 |
| Mrs. Swearingen | $20.00 |
| Mrs. Hamiltons' Co. | $22.50 |
| Woodson G. Whitt | $12.50 |
| O.F. Williams' S.S. Class | $15.00 |
| Mrs. E. Campbell | $12.50 |
| Knights of Pythias | $10.00 |
| I.O.O.F. | $ 7.25 |
| Mrs. Hills' Co. | $22.50 |
| Eastern Star | $10.00 |
| Ben Herr | $ 7.25 |
| Mrs. Hill for George | $10.00 |
| Mrs. Amanda Gooch | $10.00 |
| Miss Sallie Chinns' Co. | $80.00 |
| Miss Sallie Chinns' Co.  2/18/1910 | $15.00 |
| Mrs. Hamiltons' Co. | $50.00 |
| Mrs. Browns' S.S. Class | $12.50 |
| Home Mission Society | $22.50 |
| Smith Lodge Masons | $20.00 |
| Mrs. Huddleston | $ 5.00 |
| Mrs. Cobbs | $87.50 |
| Choir | $24.00 |
| Total to March 7, 1910 | $516.00 |

# Disbursements
# Up to March 7, 1910

| | |
|---|---|
| Bryant Bros. Art Glass Co. | $108.00 |
| F.J. Ginn, Fright on Pews | $ 29.81 |
| J. Macabee, Hauling Pews | $ 3.00 |
| J.W. Ramey, Hauling Windows | $ .75 |
| F.J. Ginn, Fright on Glass | $ 6.44 |
| John Hill, work at church | $ 5.25 |
| Haskell Lusk, work at church | $ 4.50 |
| F.J. Ginn, Express Pew Ends | $ 2.91 |
| Haskell Lusk and Guy Trent, work | $ 4.50 |
| F.J Ginn, Fright on gas Chandelier | $ 4.50 |
| J.W. Macabee, Hauling Dirt | $ 6.40 |
| Cleveland Seating Co. On Pews | $242.19 |
| Total Disbursements | $418.25 |
| | |
| Balance on hand, March 7, 1910 | $ 97.75 |
| | $516.00 |

# Methodist Episcopal Church, South
# Report of the Trustees,
### August 15, 1910

Herewith we hand you report in answer to Disciplinary Question #29.

We have one church here in Russell, which has been built at a total cost of $12,200. For the various items of expenditures, etc, see report of building committee, and witness our receipt therefore as hereto appended. The building and lot are worth $1500. ($15,000.00 ?)

We have no Insurance in force, but will soon take out a policy. The deed contains the Disciplinary Trust Clause. The title papers are kept by Mrs. Birdie Cobbs, Russell, KY. This Deed is on record in the County Clerks Office of Greenup County, KY., Deed Book #R, Page 458.

We have received from the building committee upon settlement made July 7/10, the following amounts:

| | |
|---|---:|
| Old subscription List | $ 1,520.00 |
| New subscription List | 5,601.00 |
| Check from J.W. Sutton, Tres., Gen. Fund | 9.06 |
| Check from O.F. Williams, Tres., Art Glass | 8.52 |
| Cash from General Collection Dedication Day | 32.37 |
| A Balance on Art Glass sold | 103.00 |
| A total amount from the Building Committee | $ 7,273.45 |

This amount, together with $3,078, previously collected and paid over, and $1,500.00 Loan from the Board of Church

Extension and $400.00 donation pays all our debt and gives a small surplus of $51.50.

Respectfully submitted
To Board of Trustees, by
*Thomas De Maro*

## REPORT OF THE BUILDING COMMITTEE
### AUGUST 15, 1910

We, your committee, appointed to build a Church beg to submit our final report, which is supplemental and completing to the report made to the Second Quarterly Conference current year.

We have erected the Church at a total cost of $12,200.00; this includes all the furnishings, Art Glass, Heating plant and pews.

Prior to Dedication, which was July 3, 1910, we had raised from all sources                                            $ 3,078.80
We had on hand at that date, unpaid Sub.                        1,520.00
A balance due on Art Glass                                      103.00
Raised on Dedication Day in Subscription                        5,601.00
Pledge from the Bd. Of Church Extension                         400.00
Pledge of Loan from the Bd. Of Ch. Exten.                       1,500.00
Paid over to the Treasurer Bd. Of Trustees
Cash from Dedication Day                                        31.37

On settlement with Trustees, July 7, 1910
From J.W. Sutton, Treasurer                               $      9.06
On Settlement with Trustees, July 7,1910
From O.F.Williams, Art Glass                                  8.52
A Grand Total of                                          $12,251.25

This account for all money passing through our hands, save $50.00 which amount was paid to Bishop Waterhouse, $5.00 of which we did not have, for it was handed in by Sister Clancy; the $45.00 was paid out of the Art Glass fund, which reports shows. Having completed our work, and settled with Board of Trustees, we submit herewith, New and Old Subscription list, Invoice of all bills, Treasurer's report of the General Building fund, and the Art Glass fund was held separate from the General Fund, and ask that we be relieved of all responsibility, as endorsers and else, and discharged.

> Very Truly,
> Building Committee
> M.E. Church, South
> *Thomas DeMaro, President*

# Program and Dedication

## First M.E. South
Sunday, July 30, 1910
Russell, Kentucky

## Bishop R.G. Waterhouse, D.D.
Emory, Virginia

---

## B.F. Gosling, D.D., Presiding Elder, Ashland District

---

## O.F. Williams, Pastor In Charge

# Program

Anthem..................."I Was Bled"...................Choir

Song...............................................................660

The per-fect world, by Ad-am trod;
Was the first tem-ple built by God;
His fi-at laid the cor-ner stone,
And heaved its pillars one by one. Amen

He hung its starry roof on high,
The broad expanse of azure sky;
He spread its payment, green and bright
And curtained it with morning light.

The mountains in their places stood,
The sea, the sky, a house for thee;
And when its first pure praises rang,

Lord, 'tis not ours to make the sea,
And earth, and sky, a house for thee;
But in thy sight our offering stands,
A humble temple, made with hands.

The Apostles Creed

Prayer

Anthem

Scripture Reading

Song..............................................................661

Come, O thou God of Grace,
Dwell in this ho-ly place,
E'en now des-cend!
This tem-ple, reared to thee,
O may it ev-er be
Filled with thy maj-es-ty,
Till time shall end!  Amen

Be in each song of praise
Which here thy people raise
With hearts aflame!
Let every anthem rise
Like incense to the skies,
A joyful sacrifice,
To thy blest name!

Speak, O eternal Lord,
Out of thy living word,
O give success!
Do thou the truth impart
Unto each waiting heart;
Source of all strength thou art,
Thy gospel bless!

To the great One in Three
Glory and praises be
In love now given!

Glad songs to thee we sing,
Glad hearts to thee we bring,
Till we our God and King
Shall praise in Heaven!

Sermon.........................Bishop R.G. Waterhouse, D.D.

Song...................................................................Page 666

We rear not a tem-ple, like Ju-dah's of old,
Whose por-tals were mar-ble, whose vault-ing were gold
No in-cense is light-ed, no vic-tims are slain,
No mon-arch kneels praying to hal-low the fane.  A-men

More simple and lowly the walls that we raise,
And humbler and pomp of procession and praise,
Where the heart is the altar whence incense shall roll,
And Messiah the King who shall pray for the soul.

O Father, come in!  but not in the cloud
Which filled the bright courts where thy chosen ones bowed;
But come in that spirit of glory and grace,
Which beams on the soul and illumines the face.

O come in the power of thy live-giving word,
And reveal to each heart its Redeemer and Lord:
Till faith bring the peace to the penitent given,
And love fill the air with the fragrance of  Heaven.

Benediction

# Program

Children's Day Services, Mead Memorial M. E. Church, South,
Russell, KY., Sunday Evening, July 2, 1922

Opening Song ------------------------------------------------School
Recitation—"Children's Day"------------------Virginia Grooms
Prayer---------------------------------------------------Beginners
Recitation--"All Upset"---------------------------------Ruth Perry
Recitation--"His Idea of It"--------------------------Jimmy Long
Recitation--"My Age"--------------------------Elliot Mae Hawes
Recitation--"Catching a Whale"-----------Lilly Frances Stevens
Dialogue--"Old Folks-------------Rosetta Perry, Leroy Vaughan
Recitation--"My Little Brother"--------------------Rosetta Mahle
Dialogue--"The Little Army"--Edward Bratton, Buster Arthur,
          Elmer Bratton, Chilton Long, Billy Bratton
Song--"In the Garden"------------------------------Primaries
Japanese Drill------------------------------------------Four Girls
Recitation----------------------------------------Elizabeth Mahle
Recitation----------------------------------------Katherine Leake
Recitation-------------------------------------------Dickey Grooms
Recitation--------------------------------------------Buddy Webber
Song---------------------------------------------Frances Wilson
Recitation-------------------------------------------Billy Morrow
Song----------------------------------------------------Juniors
Tableau----------------------------------------------"America"
Recitation----------------------------------------------Edyth Hyden
Recitation------------------------------------Rebecca Shepherd

Song--------------------------------------------------Dorothy Gladwell
Recitation--------------------------------------------Elizabeth Hendricks
Recitation------------------------------------------------Stella Webber
Recitation --------------------------------------------Otewha Fouts
Recitation--------------------------------------------------Frances Wilson
Recitation--------------------------------------------------Bernice Rice
Duet--Piano and Violin-----------Numa Lee Fouts, Dalton Fouts
Recitation------------------------------------------------Billy Morrow
Recitation-----------------------------------------------Faqua Hendricks
Fan Drill------------------------------------------------------Juniors
Solo-------------------------------------------------------Ruth Avis
Offering
Closing Song-----------------------------------------------School

## COMMITTEE

Mrs. C.E. Bratton, Mrs. Claro Leake, Mrs. A.D. Wilson,
Miss Sarah Waldron

## OFFICERS AND ORGANIZATIONS

## MEAD MEMORIAL METHODIST EPISCOPAL CHURCH
## SOUTH—1935

Bishop Edwin D. Mauzon, D.D., L.L.D., Charlotte,N.C.
...................................................Bishop in Charge
Rev. I.S. Tyler, Linwood Avenue, Ashland, Kentucky
........................Presiding Elder, Ashland District
Rev. Wm. H. Fogleson, D.D...................Pastor
Mrs. C.E. Bratton....................General Superintendent
Miss Sarah Marie Hardin........Pianist and Choir Director
Mrs. Elizabeth Warnick..............Assistant Pianist
Mrs. Samuel Warnick............Pianist Church School
Mrs. Edward Ballengee.........Assistant Pianist Church School
Glen Wilson....................President Young People's Division
Mrs. W.H. Foglesong....President Woman's Missionary
Society

## TRUSTEES

Dr. J.F. Wright, Curtis Smith, C.H. Stephens, H.T. Short,
D.F. Hendricks, J.D. Sweet, S.S. Hill, L.R. Dingus

## STEWARDS

C.E. Bratton, H.T. Short, Mrs. Lillie Hardin, Mrs. Alice Riel, Henry H. Hunt, Miss Sallie Chinn, Dr. J.F. Wright, D.F. Hendricks, Mrs. R.K. McCutcheon, Mrs. E.W. Smith, J.E. Frazier, C.H. Stephens, Dr. Barrett Giles.

## BOARD OF CHRISTAIN EDUCATION

W.H. Foglesong, Miss Edyth Yoak, Mrs. Alice Riel, Glen Wilson, A.H. Schmidt, Mrs, Lilly Gardin, Mrs. Barrett Giles, A.M. Lewis, Mrs. C.E. Bratton, Mrs. Lucy Leach, Miss Sallie Chinn, Mrs. W. H. Foglesong.

## WOMEN'S MISSIONARY SOCIETY

President.................................Mrs. W.H. Foglesong
Vice President..........................Mrs. E.W. Smith
Corresponding Secretary...............Mrs. S.B. Nichols
Recording Secretary....................Mrs. H.T. Short
Treasurer................................Mrs. Virginia McConahey
Secretary of Children's Work.........Miss Susan Davidson
Supt. of Baby Needs...................Miss Sallie Chinn
Supt. of Christian Social Relations...Mrs. John Peery
Supt. of Study..........................Mrs. Alice Riel
Supt. of Publicity.......................Mrs. Lucy Leach

Supt. of Supplies.........................Mrs. L.R. Dingus
Supt. of World Outlook.................Mrs. J.T. Agnew
Supt. of Local Work.....................Mrs. Mary Hill
Chairman Spiritual Life Committee....Mrs. W.A. Brown

## YOUNG PEOPLE'S DIVISION

Mrs. Barrett Giles, Adult Counselor
A.M. Church School--P.M. Epworth League

President......................................Glen Wilson
Vice President.............................Helen Ruth Hendricks
Secretary....................................Virginia Hogg
Treasurer....................................Kitty Ann Delahunt
Pianist........................................Louise Stephens
Superintendent of Publicity.................James Melvin
Representative Bd. Of Christian Education...Glen Wilson

## COMMITTEES

1. Worship, Evangelism and Church Relationship, Missions and Community Services--Edward Bratton, Chairman; Marjorie LeFlamboy, Louise Stephens, Mary Stephens, Bing Percell.
2. Citizenship and Community Service, Recreation and Personal Development, Leadership Training-George Hendricks, Chairman; Jackie Bratton, Bettie LaFlamboy, Danny Smith, James Hamer.

# CHURCH SCHOOL

## GENERAL OFFICERS

Rev. Wm.H. Foglesong, D.D…………………..Minister
Mrs. C.E. Bratton……………….General Superintendent
L.C. Brash…………………………………Secretary
James Schmidt………………..Assistant Secretary
Miss Sarah Marie Hardin…………………Treasurer

## DIVISION HEADS—TEACHERS AND OFFICERS

### CHILDREN'S DIVISION
Mrs. Alice Riel, Superintendent

TEACHERS--1. Nursery--Miss Sallie Chinn. 2. Beginners--
Mrs. J.C. Hamer, Helen Hendricks, Kathleen Brummett. 3.
Primary--Mrs. Lillie Hardin, Miss Bonnie Brummett, Miss
Sarah Hendricks, Mrs. John Perry, Mrs. Brown Mahle. 4.
Juniors--Mrs. T.E. Carmichael, Mrs. Bruce Mitchell, Mrs.
Nancy Evans, Mrs. J.D. Sweet, Miss Susan Davidson, Miss
Rebecca Angel.

### YOUNG PEOPLE'S DIVISION

Mrs. Barrett Giles, Superintendent

TEACHERS--1. Intermediates--Mrs. Curtis Smith, Mrs. Rebecca Henderson. 2. Seniors--J.E. Frazier, A.H. Schmidt, Assistant; Mrs. Elizabeth Warnick. 3. Young People--Mrs. J.F. Wright, Mrs. W.H. Foglesong, Assistant.

## ADULT DIVISION

Mrs. Lucy Leach, Superintendent

TEACHERS AND OFFICERS--1. Rail Road Men's Bible Class--B.F. Kidwell, Teacher; The Pastor, Assistant; D.F. Hendricks, President; Jack Sweet, Vice President; H.W. Riel, Secretary-Treasurer. 2. J.O.Y. Class--Miss Edyth Yoak, Teacher; Mrs. B.F. Kidwell, President; Mrs. L.R. Dingus Vice President; Mrs. Sylva Nichols, Secretary; Mrs. O.C. Cool, Treasurer. 3. Ladies Bible Class--Rev. A. J. McComas, Teacher; Mrs. W.A Brown, Assistant; Mrs. H.T. Short, President; Mrs. J.J. Rathburn, Vice President; Mrs. E.W. Smith, Secretary; Mrs. Fannie Oaks, Assistant Secretary; Miss Susan Davidson, Treasurer.

## CHURCH SCHOOL WORSHIP COMMITTEE

Mrs. Lucy Leach, Chairman; Mrs. Rebecca Henderson, Mrs. Elizabeth Warnick, Miss Sarah Marie Hardin.

## PRESENT CORNERSTONE CONTENTS, 1947

1.  Russell Newspaper, 1910

2.  Russell Newspaper, 1947

3.  Some Sunday School Roll Books

4.  Some Coins

5.  Possibly Some Paper Money

6.  A List of the Members of the Church in 1947 (185 or 251

7.  A List of the Pastors of the church from 1907 until 1947

8.  Yearbook and Directory--Mead Memorial M.E. Church, South, Russell, Kentucky, 1935-1936

9.  Report of Committee on Planning Merger of the First Methodist Church and Mead Memorial Methodist Church of Russell, Kentucky. (April 13, 1947)

# CHRISTIAN SYMBOLS FOUND IN MEAD MEMORIAL UNITED METHODIST CHURCH:

1. CROSS--Salvation
2. ARCHES--Front door-Hospitality
3. BIBLE-the Book of Books
4. PULPIT-where the Truth or Word of God is Expounded
5. FLAG-Freedom
6. SEAL-Holy Spirit
7. Harp-Joy of the most excellent things of their kind
8. TRUMPETS-Testimony or announcements
9. DOVE-peace and Holy Spirit
10. CROSS AND ANCHOR-promise fulfilled
11. ROCK AND CROSS IN WATER-safety in God's trust
12. CIRCLE OF LINKED CHAIN-safety in unity
13. SHIP AMID SEA-trust
14. EYE-all seeing
15. ARK-Church of Christ
16. ANCHOR-security, also devotion
17. SHIELD-humility and charity
18. SCROLL-written Word, whether of God or man
19. EXTENDED HAND-fellowship
20. CROWN-reward or promise
21. BEE HIVE-constancy or prepare to live
22. HYSSOP-clear and pure
23. STAR WITH FIVE DIFFERENT COLORED POINTS-worship
24. MASTER WITH LAMB-good shepherd
25. CROSS AND CROWN-victory
26. URN-immortality

27. VINE-the Word
28. GRAPES-promise of fruitfulness
29. CANDLE-light of the world
30. TRIANGLE AND THREE CIRCLES-faith, hope, and charity-Holy Trinity
31. SCALES-justice
32. OLIVE BRANCH-peace
33. LAMB-lamb of God-innocence
34. ROSE OF SHARON-Savior's flower

## STAINED GLASS WINDOWS AS THEY APPEAR IN MEAD CHURCH:

1. Far left corner of sanctuary--faith, hope, and charity--Bible at foot of cross
2. Dove with olive branch
3. Harp
4. Triangle with dove
5. Water, rock, and cross
6. Jesus with lamb
7. Crown, crusader's flag
8. Cross, crown, Bible
9. Lamp on Bible
10. Cross positioned in crown
11. Lamp holding crusader's flag
12. Choir loft;  Horn, Horn Harp

13. Downstairs hallway: Masonic symbols from the Smith Lodge

14. Upstairs hallway: Cross on blue; triangle and dove; ark. Pulpit, dove, ship tossed; Holy Grail; anchor; and open Bible

15. Upstairs classroom: hand of God; faith, hope, and charity; wheat; dove; bee hive.

16. Upstairs balcony: Masonic symbol, Eastern Star symbol lily and grape under small rosetta window; large rosetta lily and Rose of Sharon under small rosetta; Noah's ark and dove; faith, hope, and charity encircling cross and Bible on anchor. The large rosetta window is repeated at the front of the Church.

# FIRST UNITED METHODIST CHURCH

# A BRIEF CHURCH HISTORY

The First United Methodist Church dates back to the year 1870 when a Sunday School was organized in the home of Mr. and Mrs. James Rayburn. Their home stood at the corner of Main and Bellefonte Streets, where the cab stand is now located. Because of increased attendance, members were forced to find larger facilities, and they moved their services to an old log building at the foot of Amanda Hill near the bank of Bear Run, where Kenwood Blvd. runs into Route 23.

The church appears in the Journal of the Conference as an appointment for the first time in 1874. During those early years, the church was served by circuit riding preachers who traveled a large area visiting other Methodist congregations in Greenup County.

In 1887, Captain Anthony Carner gave the church a lot on Bellefonte Street between Houston and Ferry Streets. The congregation, through hard work and deep commitment, soon had a frame structure in which to worship. The first service was held in the fall of 1888, and this building was later known as "The Little White Church".

In 1908 a house was purchased on Riverside Drive that would serve as a parsonage for the families of the pastors for fifty-eight years. In 1925, a lot at the corner of Main and Etna Streets was secured and plans were under way for the construction of a larger building. Those plans culminated with the building of the present church structure and dedication services were held October 28, 1928.

A new parsonage was purchased on Audubon Court in the Kenwood area in 1966. The past four ministers have lived in this beautiful home; formal dedication of the resident was September 22, 1974. (1)

FOOTNOTE

(1) Mead Memorial Church Records. Filed under Church History.

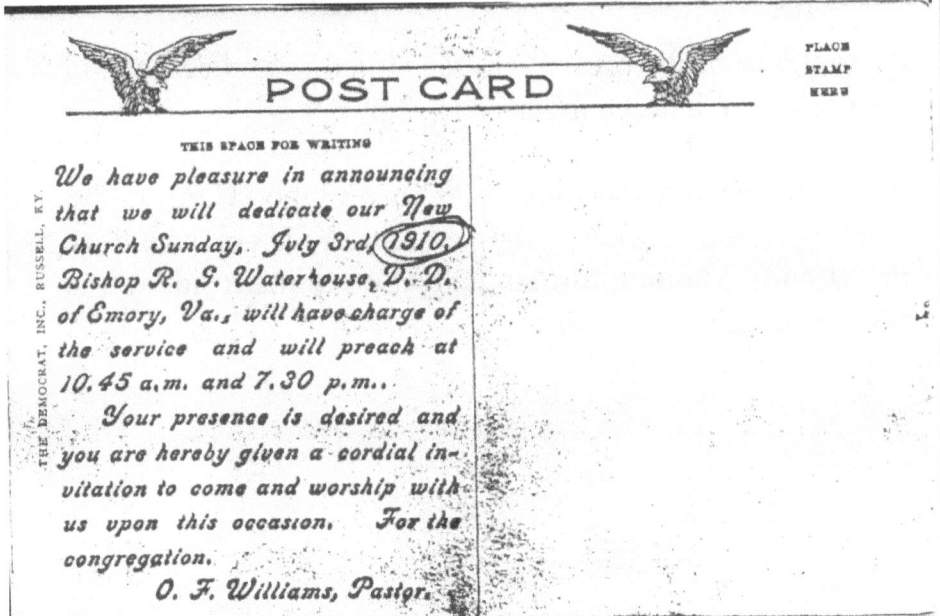

POST CARD

PLACE STAMP HERE

THIS SPACE FOR WRITING

*We have pleasure in announcing that we will dedicate our New Church Sunday, July 3rd, 1910. Bishop R. S. Waterhouse, D. D. of Emory, Va., will have charge of the service and will preach at 10.45 a.m. and 7.30 p.m..*

*Your presence is desired and you are hereby given a cordial invitation to come and worship with us upon this occasion. For the congregation.*

*O. F. Williams, Pastor.*

Postcard to showcase the new church in 1910.

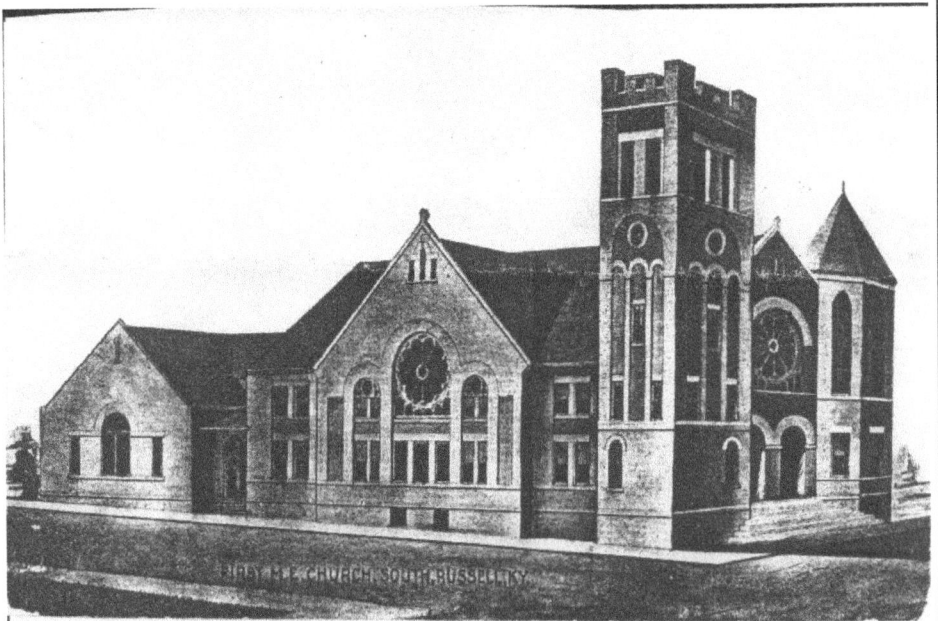

An old Fashioned Church for a New Fangled World

# MEAD MEMORIAL
# METHODIST CHURCH

**Boyd and Houston Streets**

**Russell, Kentucky**

Pastor- Ronald J. Masters

Directory for 1966-67

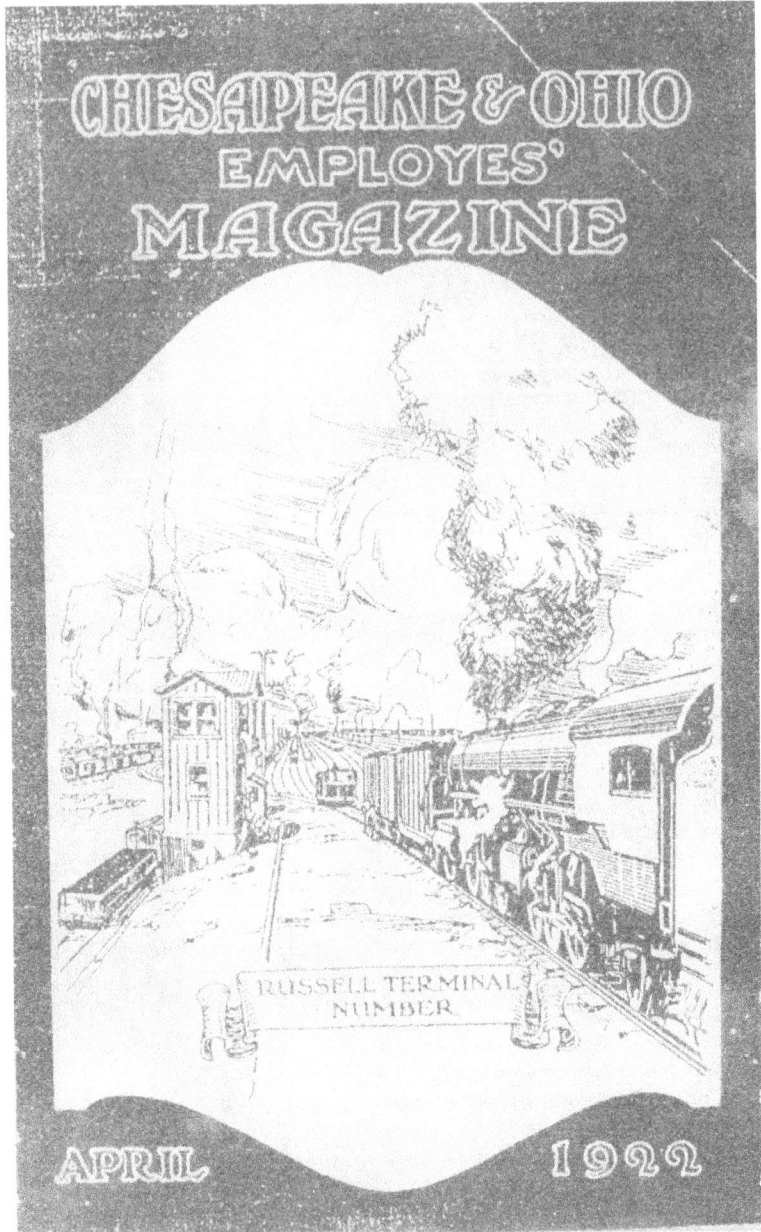

**CHESAPEAKE & OHIO EMPLOYES' MAGAZINE**

RUSSELL TERMINAL NUMBER

APRIL 1922

Since the C&O had so much to do with the church folks I added this photo.

Ironton-Russell Bridge, Notice the toll Booth is open.

The first Russell YMCA, this was about 1922 Organizes 1896

## SUNDAY SCHOOL TEACHERS AND SOME CHURCH OFFICIALS AS OF JULY, 1980

Superintendent of Sunday School  - Lillian Mckenzie

| | |
|---|---|
| Macky Meadows | Youth Sunday School |
| Wanda Nichols | Youth Sunday School |
| (Celeste McClanahan) | Substitute |
| Mary Poe | Youth Sunday School |
| Sharon Lanham | Youth Sunday School |
| Tom Bransom | Youth Sunday School |
| Mike Rankin | Single Adults |
| Debbie Meadows | Young Adults |
| Lillian Mckenzie | Adults Sunday School |
| (Gene Simpson) | Substitute |
| Teresa Mitchell | Adults Sunday School |
| (Elizabeth Poe | Substitute |
| Numia Lee Fouts) | Substitute |

Lay Leader                          Bill Lanham

Chairman of Administrative Bd. Bob Mitchell

Trustees                              Fred Caudill, Bill Lanham, Midge Lyons, Ray Shafer, Cliff Simpson

Church Treasurer            Mary Ellen Griffith

Choir Director                  Fay Pickel

| | |
|---|---|
| Pianist | Della Burton |
| Organist | Lynn Wilson Dixon |
| Ushers | Bernard King & Ray Shafer |
| Church Historians | Sarah Marie Arrington & Edith Yoak |
| Custodian | Johnny McClanahan |
| Jr. UMYF Leaders | Macky Meadows & Sharon Lanham |
| Sr. UMYF Leaders | Roger McClanahan, Celeste McClanahan, Tom Branson, & Larry Nichols |
| Softball Coach | Larry Gartin |
| Children's Sermon | Lynn Dixon, Macky Meadows, Larry Gartin. Jean Ann Caudill, Sissy Shaffer, & Larry Nichols |

**1980 BOARD MEMBERS:**

Bill Lanham,
Golda Lambert,
Lillian Mckenzie, Gladys
Simpson, Sarah Marie
Arrington, Edith Yoak, Larry
Nichols, Mary Poe, Teresa
Mitchell, Virginia Gehrling,
Mary Ellen Griffith,
Sharon Lanham,
Bob Mitchell,
Pauline Simpson,
Della Burton,
Wanda Nichols,
Numia Lee Fouts,
Carrie Harless,
Rosemond  Greenslate,
Macky Meadows,
Celeste McClanahan,
Virginia Sha
Debbie Meadows
Kelly Wells,
Elizabeth Poe,
Cliff Simpson,
Jean Ann Caudill,
Butch A. Meadows
John Hill,
Fay Pickel

## HONORARY MEMBERS OF THE ADMINISTRATIVE BOARD:

Marie Sparks, Ora Smith, Mattie Love, Mr. & Mrs. J.D. Sweet,

## MEMBERS AT LARGE OF THE ADMINISTRATIVE BOARD:

Edith Yoak, Butch Meadows, Fay Pickel, John Hill, Elizabeth Poe, Gladys Simpson, Gene Simpson, Carrie Harless, Sarah Marie Arrington,

## YOUTH MEMBERS OF THE COUNCIL ON MIMISTRIES:

Kelly Wells          Mindy Mitchell

## YOUNG ADULT MEMBERS OF THE COUNCIL ON MINISTRIES:

Mary Ellen Griffith          Francis Browning

RECORDING SECRETARY          Lillian McKenzie

COORDINATOR OF COMMUNICATIONS  Edith Yoak

SECRETARY OF CAREER PLANNING AND COUNSELING   Golda Lambert

FINANCIAL SECRETARY   Sharon Lanham

MEMBERSHIP SECRETARY   Jean Ann Caudill

REPRESENTATIVE OF THE UNITED STATES
METHODIST YOUTH MINISTRY   Mindy Mitchell

LAY MEMBERS OF THE ANNUAL CONFERENCE
Mary Poe      Fay Pickel

COMMITTEE ON NOMINATIONS AND PERSONNEL
Larry Nichols, Della Burton, Virginia Gehrling, Teresa
Mitchell, Virginia Shafer, & Debbie Meadows

CHURCH OFFICIALS CONTINUED


COMMITTEE ON FINANCE   Bill Lanham, Larry Nichols,
Mary Poe, Bob Mitchell, Lillian McKenzie, Butch Meadows,
Mary Ellen Griffith & Cliff Simpson

MEMBERS OF COUNCIL ON MIMISTRIES
Sharon Lanham, Bill Lanham, Della Burton, Lillian McKenzie,
Macky Meadows, Celeste McClanahan, Virginia Shafer,
Debbie Meadows, Golda Lambert, Pauline Simpson, Mary Poe,
Wanda Nichols, Numia Lee Fouts, Carrie Harless, Rosemond
Greenslate, Kelly Wells, & Mindy Mitchell

CHOIR MEMBERS   Mary Poe, Debbie Meadows, Elizabeth
Poe, Sharon Lanham, Tom Branson, Jenny Meadows, Carrie
Harless, Fay Pickel, Virginia Shafer,

NEW COMERS  Bernard & Debbie King, Glen & Sandy Mullins, Tom & Diana Branson, Larry & Karen Gartin, Lana & Randy Wilson, Jason & Vonnie Graham, Jim & Sandy McIntyre, Rick & Kathy Kilgore, Bill & Rita Burgess, Johnny & Anna Belle McClanahan, Floyd & Eva Hill, Johnda McClanahan, Mike Rankin, Ronald Hill, Keith & Jan Moody, Pat Scarbourgh, Bucky & Sharon Jones, Pat & Linda Franklin, Micky & Linda Fosson

SOME OF OUR YOUTH  Melissa Gallion, Steve Fannin, Chris Reeves, Matt Reeves, Bobby Herron, Kathy Hill, Scott Boggs, Mark Boggs, Richard Blevins, Michelle Fosson, Melissa Robinson, Melanie Franklin, Rusty Franklin, Mindy Mitchell, Tina Burgess, Tony Burgess, Joe Allen, Mona Allen, Tracey McKnight, Tommy McKnight, Lesi Allen, Brian Scarborough, Kelly Wells, Brenda Oney, Brenda Click, John Hite, Eric Spurlock, Mark Ellis, Terry Herron, Beth Ann Lanham, & Dalawna Meadows

POEM BY TOM BRANSON

*When time began and man was formed*
*And given life from God's own breath*
*He was not made to age with time.*
*For in the beginning there was no death.*
*But man did not obey God's law*
*And shortly after came man's fall*
*Forever banned from paradise*
*With death as punishment for us all.*
*Therefore, someday, each one must die*
*But God, in Heaven, had a plan*
*So by His love, He sent us Hope*
*His only Son to ransom man.*
*He lived God's will, as we could not*
*And blazed the trail we could not find*
*He conquered death that we may live*
*His light sent love wherever it shined.*
*And though He left, He sent His Spirit*
*To carry on what He began*
*To shine His light into earth's darkness*
*And bridge the gap 'tween God and man.*

## POEM BY TOM BRANSON

*"Step right up" the barker cried*
*"And see the things we have inside"*
*"All types of pleasure man requires"*
*"To satisfy all his desires."*
*So I, as many, stepped right in*
*Partaking of assorted sin*
*Without much thought for what I'd done*
*I reasoned it was harmless fun.*
*But soon I tired from the pace*
*And sought to exit from this place*
*The walls closed in, and darkness came.*
*I thought, I fought, and tried my best*
*To flee from my unwanted guest*
*But I was trapped within his fence*
*And he grew strong, at my expense.*
*So in despair I finally cried*
*That anyone would send a guide*
*To free me from this hollow void*
*Return a life to be enjoyed.*
*Then as the future seemed most grim*
*With my frustration at its height*
*My eyes perceived a distant light.*
*And as I ran toward the beam*
*Then I awoke, to end my dream*
*And realized that dream or not*
*An important lesson had been taught.*
*For mankind lives in darkest night, But Jesus said He is*
*The light. Yet some refuse to go His way*
*But they'll see the light on Judgment Day.*

## "The Formula For Life"
### by Tom Branson

*It's time to study mathematics*
*Let's start with man as first created*
*When made by God in His perfection.*
*Then add the sin that God so hated.*
*Perfection falls to sin's notations*
*And bliss and love give way to hate*
*And peace is trampled by aggression*
*Now man takes on a dismal state.*
*Then add a flood and its destruction*
*But add an ark to save a few*
*That God has spared from man's extinction*
*To populate His earth anew.*
*But once again we must add evil*
*To once again we must add evil*
*To spread, infect, and cause corruption*
*Within the hearts and minds of men*
*The sickness spreads in sin's eruption.*
*Now push "Sub-Total", check the numbers*
*A horrid mess, you must agree*
*For if you've added all correctly*
*A list of zero's is all you'll see.*
*Then add a tomb without a body*
*And add the man death could not hold*
*Then push the button for the total*
*And now, the answer can be told.*
*When sin was added, man eroded*
*What started whole became a fraction*
*But Jesus came to juggle figures*
*And man plus Christ is sin's subtraction.*

## WHY VOTE?

*In all the world's elections your one vote decides who wins,*
*If you do not use it wisely you will reap your every sin.*
*If you ascertain eternal truths, then victory will be yours,*
*But working hard, in your own way will bring no sure-fire*
*cures.*
*The Lord has cast His vote for you, because He loves you so,*
*He lived, and died, and rose for you, your choice is yes or no.*
*He will not force His way into your heart, against your will,*
*And yet He's voted for you, promising a better deal.*

*The devil votes against you and politics he knows.*
*He's a liar and a briar and a cheating, roaring foe.*
*He hides a wolf-like nature, wearing clothes of purest white,*
*While snatching freedom from your heart*
        *And blinding you from Light.*
*There're only three votes cast every hour of you life*
        *on earth,*
*The Lord Jesus voted for you, but the Devil wants His turf.*
        *how you'll live,*
*I recommend a yes for Christ, and real joy and peace*
        *He'll give.*

Larry S. Nichols
Harlo Press, 1975
Modern-Day Poets & Authors

# AUTOBIOGRAPHY

*Larry Sears Nichols was born in Somerset, Kentucky, on February 13, 1948, to William Raymond and Lena Sears Nichols. Mr. Nichols graduated from Somerset High School in 1966. He received his B.S. in History and Political Science from Cumberland College, Williamsburg, Kentucky, in 1969. In 1970, he received am M.A. from Union College in Barboursville, Kentucky. Additional post-graduate work has been completed at Eastern Kentucky University in Richmond, Kentucky. He has taught History and Government on the high school and college level and has also coached tennis at both levels. One year was spent as Executive Program Director of the Pulaski YMCA in Somerset, Kentucky. His published credits include one book; I'm No Appalachian Shade Tree, and a number of shorter articles and poems in various publications. He has served as pastor with seven different United Methodist churches and served as youth director at another one. Presently, he is serving as pastor of the Mead Memorial United Methodist Church in Russell, Kentucky.*

*Mr. Nichols completed his first two years of seminary education at Asbury Theological Seminary in Wilmore, Kentucky. His third year of seminary work was completed at Lexington Theological Seminary. He will graduate in May of 1980. In 1969, he married Wanda Webb from Middleboro, Kentucky. They have one son, Joshua Eric Buffalo Nichols, born October 4, 1975.*

# MEAD MEMORIAL METHODIST CHURCH PASTORS

## 1892-2011

| | |
|---|---|
| J.F. Medley | September 1892- September 1893 |
| C.W. Shearer | September 1893- September 1894 |
| J.W. Lambent | September 1894- January 1895 |
| Ernest Robinson | 1895 December 1898 |
| David H. Reid | 1898 - 1899 |
| George N. McClung | 1899 - 1900 |
| J.N. Henning | 1900 - 1902 |
| Sam Robinson | 1902 - 1903 |
| J.N. Crites | 1903 - 1904 |
| G.C. Hutchinson | 1904 - 1907 |
| O.F. Williams | 1907 - 1910 |
| Charles A. Slaughter | 1910 - 1911 |
| Percy E. Thornburg | 1911 - 1913 |
| A.A. Hollister | 1913 - 1914 |
| J.R. Mullins | 1914 - 1919 |
| H.K. Moore | 1919 - 1921 |

| | |
|---|---|
| A.L. Spencer | 1920 - 1924 |
| Ivy Yoak | 1924 - 1929 |
| John Brown | 1929 - 1931 |
| E.H. Barnette | 1931 - 1933 |
| W.H. Foglesong | 1933 - 1935 |
| C.C, Lambert | 1935 - 1938 |
| O.P. Smith | 1938 - 1944 |
| Sherwood W. Funk | 1944 - 1947 |
| R.R. Rose | 1947 - 1953 |
| J.B. Hahn | 1953 - 1956 |
| John K. Hicks | 1956 - 1960 |
| Albert Savage, Jr. | 1960 - 1964 |
| Walter Applegate | 1964 - 1965 |
| Raymond King | 1965 - 1966 |
| Ronald J. Masters | 1966 - 1967 |
| O.M. Simmerman | 1967 - 1969 |
| Paul Pepoon | 1969 - 1970 |
| Eston Calvert | 1970 - 1974 |

| | |
|---|---|
| Leonard Sumner | 1974 - 1977 |
| Ludwig L. Weaver, Jr. | 1977 - 1979 |
| Larry Sears Nichols | 1979 - 1981 |
| James W. Kemp | 1981 - 1987 |
| Larry Vickers | 1987 - 1992 |
| Donna Jones | 1992 - 1994 |
| Raymond Payne | 1994 - 2011 |
| Larry Puryear | 2011 - |

## "Let us Please God and keep this Church open another Hundred Years, Lord willing!"

## MEAD MEMORIAL UNITED METHODIST CHURCH
## ONE HUNDRED YEARS ON THE CORNER

*Mead Memorial United Methodist Church celebrates one hundred years of ministry at the present site. In 1887 a frame structure was erected at the corner of Boyd and Huston Streets. The present brick structure was dedicated July 3, 1910. A major restoration project including sanding blasting and mortar repair, window repairs and protection, and sanctuary renovations, 1981-1984, has prepared our building for another hundred years. The Boyd Street parsonage became the pastor's home in January 1985.*

*Brick and mortar are not the total story. The membership of Mead Memorial continues to grow in size and strength. The beauty of the sunlight streaming through exquisite windows is exceeded by the beauty of the Son's light radiating in folks lives. It is reflected in our worship, Sunday School, men's, women's, and youth groups. It sings in the voices of Sonrise and serves with the hands of the Country Kitchen. This light, this love, is what matters most.*

*Folks are seeking a place where they can experience an all accepting love. As Mead Memorial makes real the love of God, growth and congregational vitality will be inevitable. The future is secure in the love of Jesus Christ.*

*I give God thanks for your love and support and our chance to be part of Mead Memorial, "Where Love Matters Most."*
*Yours in Christ*
*James W. Kemp*

ADMINISTRATIVE COUNCIL FOR 2012

## OFFICERS

| | |
|---|---|
| CHAIRPERSON | JACK WEBB |
| LAY LEADER | BILL LANHAM |
| LAY LEADER EMERITUS | BOB MITCHELL |
| LAY MEMBERS TO ANNUAL CONF. | WANDA & MAC MCGAUGHEY |
| ALTERNATE LAY MEMBERS | DEBBIE & BUTCH MEADOWS |
| TREASURER | JANE WILER |
| FINANCIAL SECRETARY | DEBBIE MEADOWS |
| RECORDING SECRETARY | ADDI WHITT |
| SUNDAY SCHOOL SUPER | JEANANN CAUDILL |
| SUNDAY SCHOOL SEC/TREAS | JEANANN CAUDILL |
| CHURCH HISTORIANS | DAHNMON WHITT |
| | SHARON WHITT |
| "CALL 1" PRAYER CHAIN | GINNY MEADOWS |
| | SUZIE FIELDS |
| COMMUNION STEWARD | JIM SHOPE |
| SPECIAL NEEDS ADVOCATE | BETH GARRETT |

## COMMITTEE ON FINANCE

| | |
|---|---|
| CHAIRPERSON | PETE SMITH |
| PASTOR | LARRY PURYEAR |
| LAY MEMBER TO CONF | WANDA MCGAUGHEY |
| CHAIRPERSON AD MIN | JACK WEBB |
| LAY LEADER | BILL LANHAM |
| TRUST CHAIRPERSON | |
| FINANCIAL SECRETARY | DEBBIE MEADOWS |
| TREASURER | JANE WILER |
| SUN SCH SUP/SEC/TRES | JEAN ANN CAUDILL |

## LAY LEADERSHIP COMMITTEE

LARRY PURYEAR – CHAIRPERSON
BILL LANHAM (12)
MARY ELLEN GRIFFITH (12)
DAVID ELLIS (13)
KAREN SMITH (14)
PETE SMITH (14)
JO VIRGIN (14)

## PASTOR/PARISH RELATIONS COMMITTEE

LARRY PURYEAR - PASTOR
BILL LANHAM (12) CHAIRPERSON
JANELLE COBURN (12)
JOIE WEBB (13)
DAVID ELLIS (14)
PAT SCARBROUGH (14)
HUGH DAVIS (14)

## TRUSTEES (to elect chairperson)

SCOTT DARLING (12)
ORTHELLA DAVIS (12)
BILL LANHAM (13)
ROGER McCLANAHAN (13)
MARY ELLEN GRIFFITH (14)
GENE WELLS (14)
DICK WHITE (14)

## CHAIRPERSONS OF MINISTRY TEAMS

| | |
|---|---|
| EVANGELISM | DAHNMON WHITT |
| DISCIPLESHIP | DAVID ELLIS |
| MISSION & SCVS | PAT SHOPE |
| CHILDREN'S MIN. | BETH GARRETT |
| YOUTH MINISTRY | ADDI WHITT |
| CONG. CARE | JEANANN CAUDILL |
| WORSHIP | CATHIE SHAFFER |

## MEMBERS AT LARGE

STEVE COEBURN
DAVID WILER
CATIE PRICE
MERLE ROSE-WEST
BOB WATROUS
CAROL WATROUS

Mead Memorial
United Methodist Church
Russell, Kentucky

1987

MEAD MEMORIAL
METHODIST
CHURCH
1887 — 1909

*Restoration Begins*

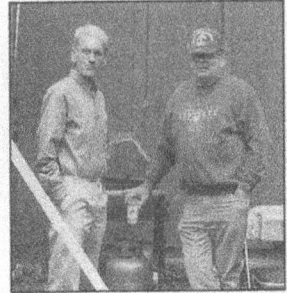

Jim Shope & Chuck Martin

The
Tower
gets a
Roof

Jim Shope handled the monies and direction, Chuck Martin supervised and did the hands on work with much help from the men of the church. This was started in the early 2000's.

*Fund Raising Activities*

**Wanda, Jane, Macky & Sissi helping**

**An Annual Event at Mead**

The ladies of the church raised funds for restoration.

Our Vision
We seek, with God's help, to be a "Church of the Good Shepherd": A family of faith, gaithered in the name of Jesus Christ, reaching out to a hurting world in love and service.

Our Mission

To make disciples of our Lord Jesus Christ: To the end that each person might become a part of God's loving purposes in his/her life, family, community, and world.

Mead Memorial United Methodist Church
501 Boyd Street, PO Box L
Russell, Kentucky 41169
(606) 836-6247
www.meadmemorial.org

In the 4th century A.D. St. Augustine wrote these words, "You have made us for yourself, O Lord, and our hearts are restless until they find rest in You".

At Mead Memorial United Methodist church we believe these words reflect a profound truth about the human condition; namely, all of us have a deep need to be connected with God. We need to know God, to experience His love for us, to find forgiveness for our sins, to receive the gift of salvation He offers each of us. Until we ask God into our hearts, we will always feel empty and unfilled.

We believe that the church is a family of faith and that it is within the life of the church that people can discover their need for God and enter into a life-giving, heart-changing, soul-saving relationship with Him. We believe that within the life of the church every follower of the Lord Jesus Christ can find the support, encouragement, and training he/she and their family need to live out their faith even in difficult times. We believe that within the life of the church each individual should have the chance to explore opportunities to serve God and become instruments of His grace in the larger world around us.

We believe that God's grace is truly amazing and should be a source of joy. We believe Christians, of all people, should smile. We believe that worship should celebrate the glory of God, comfort us when we need comforting, confront us with our need for God, and challenge us to grow as disciples of our Lord Jesus Christ, and strengthen us to live as witnesses for Christ in our everyday lives.

## Opening Page from the 2009 Directory

## Interview with Bill Lanham, September 2011

**Larry Sears Nichols** was a strong evangelistic type pastor, and ended up being an Evangelist for the Kentucky Conference after leaving Mead Memorial in 1981 and served in other churches.

People really admired him. He was talented and excelled in the sport of tennis. He was on fire for the Lord and had several converts.

The church had an attendance of 90 to 100 during his time as Pastor. He baptized many converts with the help of Bill Lanham. The used the waters of the Ohio River and the First Baptist Church baptistery.

**Jim Kemp** enjoyed playing a clown which thrilled the youth of the church. He loved climbing ladders. He loved to travel around downtown Russell and talk to the people. He had MS. Attendance fell off some because of his condition with Multiple-Sclerosis.

He challenged the church in a farce. He had a police officer come into the church and confiscate the Bible.

**Larry Vickers** was a devout Christian and loved to spend time alone with God. He would lie in the church floor and talk to God while looking up at the cross. He was a very serious about his preaching. Attendance was 70 to 80 under his tenure.

Next was Pastor **Donna Jones** to minister to Mead Church. She was very stern and even fired the Sunday School Superintendent. Some folks felt she was sent to the church by the District Superintendent to close it down so the flock would go to the new Grace UMC at Raceland, KY. At any rate morale and spirit was low at Mead when she left in 1994.

**Raymond Payne**

Raymond Payne, his sweet wife Peggy and their sons came to an unhappy church in June of 1994. The congregation was well pleased for the change in which a new minister could bring.

Raymond was sent to Mead Memorial by God, and it was just what the church needed. Raymond had a calming effect on the church and he was quickly loved by the congregation.

Raymond must have done a lot right, because the people of Mead Memorial kept him around for seventeen years.

Through praying to God, Raymond felt it was time to take another charge and congregation under his wing.

**Larry Puryear** and his sweet wife Linda came on June 27, 2011.

*I, Larry Puryear, follow Rev. Raymond Payne who was reappointed to another congregation after 17 years of ministry at Mead Memorial United Methodist Church. The transition has gone very well. The congregation has accepted the change in pastor's very well. I could not have been received any warmer than they have received me. I found the church's music programs to be one of the best programs in my 35 years of ministry. Along with the music program I found that the community had an active United Methodist Men's group along with two active women's groups. The newsletter is outstanding with the help of several lay members.*

*The church did have a financial obligation to pay in full the previous pastor's pension payments of some $14,000.00. They have begun to fulfill that obligation. There was also an issue with the Conference and district benevolences which the church has begun to correct. The church's other financial obligations are in order and currently the church runs a surplus in donations including a generous gift of $35,000.00 given by a lay member. Average attendance is around 60-65.*

*I have conducted one funeral and celebrated one wedding in my 5 months at this congregation. There have been neither baptisms nor any additions to membership. Two members were transferred to another Methodist Congregation.*

*I have been well pleased with my appointment to Mead Memorial United Methodist Church from June 27, 2011 to present.*

This book is dedicated to all the Saints that has gone on before and have kept this Old Church open and alive for way over 100 years. May the Lord use this book for His work and may the Lord bless all that read it.

I must mention our extra friendly Congregation. As soon as you walk in the door at Mead Memorial United Methodist Church, you feel welcome and will most assuredly want to come back.

We have a talented Musical group led by **Cathie Shaffer**. We have a great piano player, **Cindy Arthur**. We have a talented Organist, **Merle Rose-West**, which can play anything she has heard.

We have great teachers and great leadership that strives to serve the Lord Jesus Christ.

# *Come for a Visit!*

*501 Boyd Street*

*Russell, KY 41169*

*Website:*

*www.meadmemorial.org*

## *Church For A New Fangled World"*

*Sharon Whitt, Collector and Author*

*An Old Fashioned Church for A New Fangled World!*

*Mead Memorial United Methodist Church*

*Russel Kentucky*

Sharon Cogan Whitt worked as Church historian and put together this book. She is a native of Flatwoods, KY, went to Russell High School. She is a Kentucky Colonel and has been very civic minded. She has served as president of one of Kentucky's largest schools and been active in church work as this book will show. All proceeds from the book go to Mean Memorial United Methodist Church.

She was very interested in the history of this old church so she wrote a book about it. It will have special meaning to the try-state area.

Go to http://dahnmonwhittfamily.com/ to see other Publications by Dahnmon Whitt Family Publishing.

## Sharon Cogan Whitt

A description of *"An Old Fashioned Church for a New Fangled World"*. This book is about the historic church located on Boyd Street in Russell, KY. This old church has been rattles daily by the trains and has stayed open for way over 100 years through floods and perils. I talk about beginnings a grand revival in 1907 when over 200 people gave their lives to Christ. I talk about the dedication of the new church in 1910. The 1937 flood which really rocked the Ohio Valley is also mentioned in this book. The church had a mystery artist which left 3 beautiful murals in a large downstairs classroom. The church is adorned with many beautiful stained glass windows which were donated by many past members as a lasting monument to the church and the Lord. Many past church records and members are mentioned. Many old pictures of the old church and points around Russell, KY are in the book. A list of the past and present pastors that has/is serving the Lord and charge is found in this book. A dedications given to the Saints that have served God and kept Mead Memorial United Methodist Church open for over 100 years.